MARINE SPECIAL OPEF

THE INTERPRETER'S WAR

AHMED AZIZI
JIL PLUMMER

Andrew Benzie Books
Martinez, California

Published by Andrew Benzie Books
www.andrewbenziebooks.com

Printed in the United States of America
First Edition: October 2019

10 9 8 7 6 5 4 3 2 1

Azizi, Ahmed
The Interpreter's War: Marine special operations in Afghanistan

ISBN: 978-1-950562-16-9

Cover and book design by Andrew Benzie
www.andrewbenziebooks.com

I dedicate this book to my fallen hero brothers.

We few, we happy few
We band of brothers
For he today who shares his blood with me
Shall be my brother.

—Shakespeare

CONTENTS

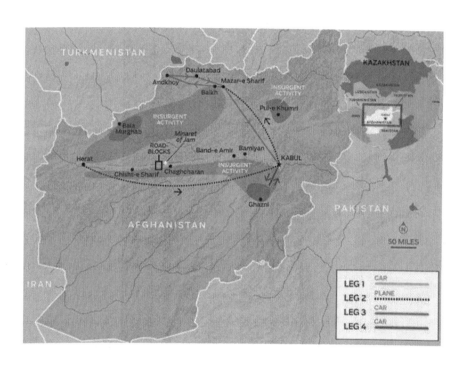

FOREWORD

LZH-Interpreter Edition Super

The war in Afghanistan began on April 1978 when the people's democratic party of Afghanistan took power in a military coup known as the Saur revolution. Most of Afghanistan experienced this uprising against the Government and the Soviets joined in December 1979 as they wanted to replace the existing communist Government with their own. Afghanistan resistance forces, known as the mujahedeen, fought against the communists. Some factions received support from other countries like the United States. Pakistan and Saudi Arabia became the middlemen.

CHAPTER 1
BEHOLD FOR MORNING IN THE BOWL OF NIGHT HAS THROWN THE STONE THAT SENDS THE STARS TO FLIGHT

The day was barely awake, the sky still dark as I awoke in my comfortable bed with my two brothers right next to me. I was thinking about the coming hours and expecting them to be like those of any other day, but what lay ahead turned out to be life changing.

I walked down the hallway to the bathroom that had a faucet we could use for only a certain amount of time before it was considered wasting valuable water. I walked back to my room where my youngest brother Khaled was putting on a fresh set of clothes and my other brother, Yama, was sitting on the bed anxious to fix his kite so he could get out and kite-fight with friends and neighbors. My mom, a teacher, in a rush to get to school shouted, "Breakfast is ready!"

We raced down the hallway, seeing who could get there first then I remember my brother Khaled saying, "What's that noise?" And my brother Yama saying, "I don't know."

We stopped short, listening, shocked to hear kids high voices shouting and parents screaming. What was happening?

My dad, an airline attendant manager, due for a flight later in the day, rushed into the living room where we were, "They're here!" he said in a hoarse voice, "The Russians are here!"

I looked out and saw enormous tanks everywhere, rumbling and crushing the pavement into dust. What was happening? We ran outside and now there were soldiers marching down my street. Their boots echoed. Thump! Thump!

Dad grabbed my shoulder. "Don't get close!"

"Stay behind us," said Mom pulling my arm.

Dad whispered something to my mom but I couldn't hear what he said. There was so much noise; engines, shouting and those boots! My brothers and I watched as Dad went to one of the Russian tanks and started talking to the soldier gunner who was on top. I could see they weren't understanding each other by the wild way they waved their hands around but then, of course, I realized the man on that tank was talking in Russian and my dad in Farsi. That was the first time I thought how important it would be to have an interpreter there for them. Suddenly the man reached down into a sack he was carrying and gave my dad a few cans of food.

At this point we brothers and my mom were even more confused. We couldn't figure out whether all this uproar was friendly or dangerous.

My dad came back and said, "Let's go inside."

So we did, and we started questioning him. Me asking, "Are they friendly?"

"Are we going to be ok?" my brother Yama kept repeating in a small scared voice.

A rushing sound came from down the hall.

"Quick, go hide behind the counter," whispered my dad as he took out the BB gun he'd brought home from his last flight to Europe.

We all crouched, hiding, scared. Afraid to breathe.

The bathroom door opened and there stood my oldest brother Wais, the toilet flushing behind him. Relief jolted us out of our hiding spot and we leapt up cheering and laughing.

"What's going on?" Wais looked completely confused.

Dad explained to him, but then told us all to not trust anyone because at this point no one knew what was really going on.

We stayed inside, not looking out until all the tanks and shouting had gone away, leaving the street quiet and empty.

We didn't go to school that day but on the next the streets seemed normal and as we saw other kids heading off with their books, Mother figured that whatever it was that happened was over and, with orders to go straight there and back, we set off.

Mother may have thought everything had gone back to normal but we kids soon realized nothing had as we passed great tanks, lurking like monsters at every corner. A voice called to us from one, in a strange guttural language. We stopped and saw a youngish looking guy beckoning to us from an open hatch. We knew not to go over, after all her warnings mother would kill us if we did. The soldier threw something and a shower of candy bars scattered at our feet. The foreigner laughed as we picked them up, tore off wrappers and stuffed sweet chocolate into our mouths. The school bell rang from several blocks away and we ran toward it.

CHAPTER 2
FIRST DEATH

Each day was the same. The nice Russian guys in the tanks gave us candy so we weren't afraid of them anymore, in fact we looked forward to our walk to school and were rather proud to have the monster tanks as our friends. We didn't tell our parents though; we just felt something wasn't right.

There was no school on Saturday and as she usually did, Mother sent me to the local pastry shop to bring some delicious warm buns back for breakfast. The tanks still lurked although I heard the clanking roar of one moving on a neighboring street and wondered if my Russian soldier was on it instead of in his usual spot.

I entered the cozy, sweet smelling warmth of the shop and, as there was a customer in uniform ahead of me, I went to the glass case to pick out what I would buy. The one with raisins was my favorite.

My coin purse clattered to the floor as I dropped it, startled by the gust of cold air as the shop door burst open. Before I could turn around an explosion deafened me and the customer crumpled to the floor. He twitched, then was still and I watched in horror as a river of blood gushed from what was left of the back of his head. I stared frozen as a couple of candy bars slid from the Russian's greatcoat. A sound made me glance toward the door as the killer slammed it behind him. For a moment he looked back and caught my eye: I recognized a neighbor from the next building to ours.

The shop owner ran around the counter and covered the dead soldier's head with a towel. "Go home," he said to me. "Go home, boy. But don't tell anyone what you saw."

And I ran, as fast as I could go, blind to everything. When I reached home I ran straight up stairs and flung myself across my bed, deaf to Mother calling my name. I felt chilled and began to shake, unable to get rid of that image of my first corpse. And then I cried.

I took a different route to school after that but things were happening there too. In fact everything was changing everywhere which was both exciting and scary. Firstly the roads were all torn up by the tanks so any normal traffic had to creep slowly and carefully instead of rushing and blowing horns as was usual. Also the air was filled with exhaust fumes whenever a tank moved and in my mind that became the smell of Russia. At school each day one period was replaced by a new teacher who taught politics, which turned out to be all about how wonderful Soviet communism was compared to the kind Afghanistan had.

Army trucks began sometimes to bring soldiers to interrupt class and take some of the older school boys, who weren't wearing the official school badge, away with them to join the army. Once I forgot to wear my ID and they arrested me on my way to school but as I was obviously under age they let me go. It scared me though, and I never forgot my badge again.

People were getting all riled up and there were student marches which I was too young to join or really understand but when I heard my parents talking about people who were picked up and never heard from again I got really scared and took special care not to be noticed. People who had long been friends and neighbors got into big arguments and began to hate each other. Colorful kites no longer played in Kabul's sky.

Some of my uncles and relatives left Afghanistan. The war was gaining momentum. Cousins who had been taken in by the army were killed and the news had adults weeping which scared us kids even more than the noise of gunfire which became louder and closer by the day. Helicopters flew overhead and I hid thinking they were looking for me. My oldest brother Wais was one of those kids at school who was chosen to join the army so my dad, who knew important people through his airline job, immediately got him a passport and sent him off to India.

He had just left when one day I stepped out of my house into the ear splitting clatter of bullets. It was chaos as from the corner I heard soldiers yelling. An Afghan, who I learned later had just killed three Government officials, was being chased by four Russian soldiers. He turned the corner onto my street, saw me and ran past into my yard. I watched him climb my wall into the neighbor's but in the process he dropped his gun and jacket with all his ammunition. The soldiers hadn't seen him turn and were busy searching the streets so, although I didn't know what was going on, I knew it was important for me to hide that man's possessions. Quickly I ran to them, grabbed a shovel and buried everything.

The neighborhood went quiet again.

Weeks later I saw government trucks stop in front of my house. Soon there was strong knocking on our door. "Stay back," said my dad and, after making sure I was out of sight, he opened up.

Through a crack I watched a soldier talking to my father and behind him, as I looked closer and closer, I saw the man who had jumped my wall, handcuffed in one of the trucks.

The soldier was speaking bad Farsi but I could understand and I stopped breathing as he told my dad, "Your son helped this man escape and he dropped his gun in your house."

Of course my father denied knowing anything about this but the soldier angrily accused him of lying. "Bring me the boy. I arrest him and will take him to jail."

"No, take me," said my dad, and to my horror I watched them take him away and could do nothing about it. I ran to my mom and through tears told her what had happened.

Quickly she snatched up the phone and made a few calls to my dad's friends in the government. To everyone's relief he got released, and later in the day we all cheered his homecoming; but at the same time I wondered what happened to the man in the truck who had no influential connections to save his life.

CHAPTER 3
INDIA

Circumstances weren't getting better on the streets of Kabul. I remember one day I looked up into the hazy sky to watch a loud jet maneuvering like in an air show. Down it went, nose first to the ground and pulled up at the last second doing flips and tricks. I knew it was the Russians showing off their power and precision.

After much discussion my parents decided they had no choice but to send me off to India. I didn't mind because I was excited to be able to see my brother Wais again.

A few weeks later I was on the plane, My dad's friend, Khan, picked me up from Gandhi International airport and I immediately looked around for Wais. "Where is my brother?" I asked searching for him amongst the swarming mass of people.

My dad's friend responded by grabbing my two suitcases off the carousel and saying, "The smugglers sent him to the U.S."

My heart sank. Seeing my brother was all I had looked forward to.

"Come on, let's get home for dinner," said Mr. Khan. "They're all looking forward to meeting you."

I soon got over the shock of Wais not being there for, as my father's friend reminded me of Robert Dinero one of my favorite movie stars, I immediately liked him, and when we reached his house and I was welcomed by his wife, a sweet, kind lady, and their three friendly boys, one my age who immediately showed me his new bicycle and let me ride it, I had no room to be homesick.

I stayed with the Khan family for a year having little contact with my family but I loved India, going to school where I took English classes, played soccer and continued Taekwondo at which I excelled, even winning competitions. The Indian people were very kind so I quickly learned Hindi. Different languages always came easily to me and I found I could switch from one to another without a thought.

My dad later told me that he sent my mom and my brothers through Pakistan hoping they would end up in India with me and then, since my dad was an airline attendant, he arranged to work a flight to India where he would stay and hopefully our family would be reunited.

Everything worked out as he planned and I could hardly believe it when I met them all in New Delhi. In fact I couldn't help hugging everyone over and over I was so happy to see my family alive and together again.

We couldn't stay here long so a few days later my dad took us to the US embassy to apply for political asylum. Weeks later we were called in by the judge for an interview and since my dad had worked for an airline and my uncle and grandmother were already in New York, we were granted permission to come to the United States of America.

CHAPTER 4
A NEW LIFE

A few weeks later we were booked on a flight to America. The day we were to leave my dad said, "Pack your bags, we have a journey ahead of us." My brothers cheered, happy to get away from our crowded rooms but I was sad to leave the Indian family who had been so kind to me; and I would miss all the friends I had made at school. This had become my home.

Our first stop after leaving New Delhi was Thailand, then we caught another flight to Hong Kong where we stayed one night in a hotel. The next day we flew from Hong Kong to Tokyo and at this point we were so tired of flying, I and my brothers were bored and grumpy. My brother, Yama, at one time said, "Dad, why is the world full of Asians?" then we all laughed and felt lighter for a few moments.

From Tokyo we took the longest flight to San Francisco and when we arrived and I got my first look at that city I said, "Wow this place is beautiful!" But we only had one night there and next day we flew to New York, our final destination, where my uncles and aunts were at the airport waiting for us. My first impression of that great city, even at the airport, was the smell of pizza on every corner.

Wais was in jail for fourteen months due to his smuggled entry into the U.S. with no passport but he got released shortly after we arrived so our family really was all together now. It was the summer of 1984 and I started working in my uncle's deli in Manhattan. Shortly after, my Dad and Uncle purchased a restaurant, thanks to the money my dad made selling our house back in Afghanistan. "Sarducci" was on 16th St. and 7th avenue and my brother, Yama, and I quit the job back in the deli to work there. I loved talking to the customers, many of whom were celebrities like Arnold Schwarzenegger and Brooke Shields, although I often didn't recognize them until someone told me later who they were. However one of my favorite people was our Mexican delivery man who knew no English so I learned a good bit of Spanish from him and found it useful in dealing with our Spanish speaking customers

Later that summer, school started so I went to High School each day, then after classes, took the subway to Manhattan to work the night shift. I was only catching four hours of sleep a night for the next two years but I was proud that our restaurant became a hit and we were known as one of the best pizza shops in Manhattan.

Two years later my Dad flew to San Francisco to see one of his cousins and he fell in love with that city, from the weather to the people. Once again he decided to move. He and Wais went first and opened a video store, then Mom and my two younger brothers followed while I stayed in New York until I finished high school so was the last one to eventually move to California.

My family were all doing well. At this time my oldest brother Wais got married. Yama made it into UC Davis, Khaled got accepted into chiropractic school and I was always working to support my younger brothers in getting their degrees.

Then in 1996, one of my second cousins, a girl, came from Germany. Our family hinted that we should marry but I ignored them. Nevertheless we slowly began to hang out, and I fell in love with my soon to be wife Rashida. I remembered that we had actually known each other when we were kids, so our relationship went way back, all the way to before times of war. We had a big engagement party after which she returned to Germany to finish college as a dental hygienist. When she returned it was to stay.

We had an extravagant, beautiful wedding. I was perfectly happy knowing she was the one I wanted to be with for the rest of my life. We spent a gorgeous honeymoon in Hawaii. Both of us coming from the same country we had never seen a place so beautiful. We stayed there for a full week: Hang gliding off the cliffs, swimming in the crystal clear waters and dining on exotic foods.

We came back and rented an apartment we called home. Rashida got a job with Western Dental and, with me working with my brothers on our car lot, we were both employed full time and would spend late nights watching movies and cuddling under the blanket with a bowl of popcorn. Life was good!

Then in 2003 something amazing - a miracle happened! We had a baby boy! We were so blessed to become Mom and Dad of our baby, Ilyas. We brought him home from the hospital to our apartment in his cute baby blue clothing and before long it seemed, he was crawling then running.

So in 2005 we bought our first house and Ilyas's second birthday was held in our new home. We had more space to enjoy our parenting and would throw big parties almost every weekend.

Then in 2007, disaster struck and our house got foreclosed on due to bad loans we were given on the mortgage. Ilyas was six now and a big boy. I felt pressure to find a better job with a higher salary. We rented a condominium to hold us during this time and always I was stressed, thinking of new ways to make money; answering ads, signing up at agencies. Each day I studied the newspaper for ideas and always the headlines told of the terrible war going on in Afghanistan. One day the main article told of a terrorist bombing in Kabul and I remembered when the Russians came to our street and how my father was trying to communicate with the Russian soldier in his tank and me, as a young boy, thinking how good it would be to have someone to interpret for them. Could I do that?

I could speak four languages fluently…

I rushed to do research and found there was a branch of the military for Interpreters. It offered good pay and a lot of tests to be taken before being accepted but I knew I could do it. I broached the idea to my wife and she was excited by the money. I must admit to being a little disappointed that she didn't seem upset at my being away and in mortal danger. My mother, however, was horrified! "What are you thinking, Ahmed? You could be killed! Or terribly injured. We left Afghanistan to save you from all that! To leave your wife and son… Please think about it!"

But I had made up my mind and besides my wife was proud of my plan and had told all our friends.

I applied to Mission Essential Personnel and took courses with them in Pleasanton, California. We were not taught a lot: mainly that we must always be on alert, eyes and ears open, ready to report anything we saw or heard to our superiors but never tell anything to the enemy. (Which seemed rather obvious to me!) In general, besides our work, we were to interpret culture and spread good will toward Americans. I also took a short course to sharpen my Pashto and after a few weeks passed all my exams.

A short time later I went to Baltimore for a week of processing after which I came back home and waited to be cleared on the background check. I waited and waited, losing hope and feeling desperate. Then suddenly I got a call and the man said, "You're getting deployed."

On the day I left, my wife threw a big farewell celebration with every family member and friend there for my departure and last party. I said goodbye to everyone, my wife wished me luck and gave me a big kiss. My little seven year old boy, Ilyas, was too small so I got down on one knee and said, "Dad will be home soon." I explained to him why I had to go but I promised to come back. He started crying, throwing a tantrum, and holding onto my neck shouting, "Don't go! Don't go!" One last big hug and I bolted out of the room and left to catch my plane to Baltimore.

CHAPTER 5
THE LONG WAIT

That night in a Baltimore hotel I had trouble sleeping, nervous about the physical tests and further exams ahead of me. What would I do if they didn't take me now? What was I letting myself in for if they did? With all the hurdles to climb to get here had I really thought of the end result? War! Did I want to be in the middle of a war? How could I promise my little son I would return?

First thing the next day I bought a million dollar life insurance policy made out to my wife and boy, then joined our hopeful group of interpreters to face an important interview. I had dressed well and when my turn came went into the room nervous and clenching my fists. Everything from now on would be an unknown journey, but all went well and I was told that next morning we, who were accepted, were going to Fort Benning, Georgia. At least I would enjoy the bus ride with fellow Interpreters.

It took thirteen hours to arrive at the military base and its Combat Readiness Center where the Mission Essential Personnel Manager was waiting to give us a briefing. "You men have a week here on base, before being deployed to modern day hell." That's what he said but I don't think any of us really believed it... then.

We were directed to our barracks and told that next day we would go to the military hospital for vaccinations. This made me nervous because of my allergy to needles, and sure enough, when the time came, after the fourth shot I fainted.

The day after that, after getting no sleep on my bed which had more like a pile of rocks than a mattress, we had another briefing, this time about awareness. They lay a blood covered doll down in front of us and demonstrated how to help an injured person. I know some interpreters quit right there because of how gruesome it was but that didn't bother me nearly as much as the shots I'd had the day before.

That awareness training took the whole day, but on the next we were issued our gear which I had been looking forward to, wondering what I would get. First we were each given three huge duffle bags and then we spent hours in a big room collecting everything we may possibly need in the days ahead from boots and body armor to sleeping bags, one for cold weather and one for hot. I asked a supervising officer where I could get my dog tags. For a second he looked puzzled then shrugged and told me not to worry. "Probably in Bahgram," he said.

It took hours to assemble everything, and then we were released to lug it all back to the barracks and stuff everything into the duffle bags. Our training was over.

Next morning an MEP driver took us to a motel where we must wait to be deployed overseas. There was a big group of us and most days several guys' names were called and they left, but for me it became a nightmare because I had to wait almost two months. Two months of longing for my wife and little boy, being bored to death and wondering what on earth I was doing here.

Stories kept circulating about how often interpreters were getting killed in Afghanistan, some having only just arrived. I tried not to think about that and with a new friend organized a Pashto class for every morning after the manager's daily briefing. That helped time pass but afternoons were long. Some of us played cards or watched TV: always I waited for mail call and my heart lifted when a letter came from home, sometimes with a small crayon drawing done by Ilyas.

The motel became more and more depressing as I waited every day until darkness fell and still no orders came. Other Translators came and went. I imagined I was forgotten. Then came a morning when the MEP manager called out, "Ahmed Azizi you are going to Afghanistan as a CAT 1."

I replied, "Fine, just get me out of this place."

Next day I received my tickets and, as I was due to leave early the following morning, I packed my gear, said goodbye to a few friends and went to bed looking forward to whatever came next.

Another guy named Peyman and I went by shuttle to Atlanta Airport. From there we took a flight to Washington Dulles, and a seven hour layover. Since Peyman lived there his family came to see him for the last time and they took us to their house for a meal, treating me like their own. Later they gave us a ride back to the airport, and we got on our flight, Qatar Airlines nonstop to Qatar.

During the flight I got talking to the Interpreter next to me. There was something familiar about him, maybe the very blue eyes and American look of him despite his accent being definitely Afghan. To our mutual surprise we discovered we were both born in the town of Karteparwan and had played together as children. His name was Saffi and it was like meeting a brother .

We talked until the plane landed in Qatar where a Mission Essential Personnel representative met us and took us to the U.S. military base and into the Translator tent where the temperature was not far from boiling.

And there we waited, sweating, for another couple of days, with only a few desultory wanderings through the nearby bazaar before catching our flight on a C17 Airplane to Baghian Airfield Afghanistan.

CHAPTER 6
BOOTS ON THE GROUND

It felt like an earthquake when the C17 rose its wings and took off into the thin air bound for Afghanistan. Three hours later we touched down in Baghian Airfield. The whole back of the plane opened and a soldier ushered us out. When I stepped off and my foot touched the ground, I couldn't believe it; after more than quarter of a century I was back in my homeland. Although I no longer held Afghan citizenship I filled with emotion as I stood, taking in the beautiful familiar mountains. I filled my lungs with air exactly the same as I remembered. Yes, I was home!

We lined up for a briefing and then an MEP driver drove us around the base to this huge Interpreter's Tent, commonly called the Terp tent. We still had to carry our luggage and duffle bags and I was sweating and my shoulders aching by the time I got inside and saw the bunks lined up one after another in long rows, There were so many translators that at first I couldn't find a bottom bed as I had quickly decided I definitely did not want a top one, but finally there it was right at the end of a row. With relief I dropped my load and sat down on the edge of the wafer thin mattress.

An extraordinary deafening roar suddenly shook the whole tent. It rumbled like an earthquake making me want to cower and hide, then it was gone. It took a moment for me to realize it was an F16 jet taking off. I would have to get used to such things.

There must be food somewhere but I was too tired and just stretched out and slept fully clothed beside my belongings.

In the morning we awoke and, as would become routine, an MEP representative gave us a briefing. This day we would be bused to an

MEP office to put our names into the system so they could manage our time both in the field and going back home. At the office I asked again for my dog tags. The clerk looked at me over her glasses. "Only military personnel get dog tags. You are a contractor. Please move on."

I was mad. They gave me body armor, obviously to be used in dangerous situations, yet I get nothing to identify my dead body? A lot of good my new life insurance policy would be. I immediately invested in a dozen of the best black markers I could find and that night wrote my ID on every piece of government issue clothing in my duffel.

Some interpreters spoke nervously about hearing that a group of people had gotten their assignments for the next day. Everyone was wishing to be sent to one of the safer parts of Afghanistan and when I went to see if my name was up, there it was, "To Herat with special ops." People said "Wow, you're lucky! Herat's a safe place." But I had wished to be assigned to work in Baghian and Kabul.

So we went back to the tent that night after a decent meal and the only sound was the roar of F16's taking off and landing. The place was like a war zone and I had just gotten to sleep when I was awakened by sirens and loud rumbles. Someone came in and told us we had been attacked by rockets on the other side of the base and there were several casualties. He said it was chaos over there with people trying to douse a fire and medics rushing to the scene, carrying injured out. So, I guessed, every place really was a war zone from here on.

At 3 a.m. Movement guys, which was the name we gave them because they were always moving us from one place to another, awoke me with orders that I had to catch a flight to Herat. I got out of bed and onto my still sleeping feet. Seeing everyone packing their gear I hurried to start on my own, nervous but glad to get on with whatever lay ahead.

A shuttle took us to the side of a terminal where the military planes were stationed and we were marched to the tall, proud standing C 130 that had its back open, waiting for us. No sooner had we found our seats, that were as hard as our beds, than we took off steeply and as soon as we gained altitude we were already descending to our first stop—Kabul.

We waited while they spent a few hours emptying out cargo and some military personnel then, after refueling, we took off and I was looking down at my birthplace through the foggy small window of the C 130, thinking how twenty-nine years before I had escaped this city for a better life.

A couple of hours later we landed in Herat and deplaned to the sight of six military trucks waiting to take us to the base which was ten minutes away. There an MEP representative led us to a transit tent where I got probably my hundredth briefing then was taken next door to the Special Forces portion of the base and to the tent with other translators. We were assigned foldable beds and I was ready for mine. Movement guys told me there was an Italian pizza shop where they went every night, which was encouraging. Evidently each team had a different food preference, for example: MARSOC members would usually barbecue. Most of the guards were Afghan so I made a point of striking up conversations with them to hear all the most recent rumors. Many of these turned out to be like the first I heard about a translator who had been burned alive while he was in Herat. The guards liked to talk about that kind of thing, maybe because I was new and they wanted to scare me, but I didn't believe most of it. Besides my friend Staffi had been assigned to Herat and I'd just seen him off that morning.

It was nice that we could wash up and take showers and get nice meals here, but what was about to happen wouldn't be as pleasant.

I was sitting on my cot when a guy in charge of interpreters on the base came in and said, "You are going to Bala Murghab."

After he left everybody was staring at me and one guy said, "Wow, you're going to Bala Murghab." Some others said that I should just quit right now because of how terrifying and deadly that place was. I didn't know anything about it but I didn't sleep as well that night as I'd expected.

"Where is Azizi?" It was early next morning and when I replied, "I'm Azizi." Jay, a friendly-seeming black American in Special Forces uniform, introduced himself and said, "Let's go." I dressed quickly and a few other translators mumbled, "Good luck," as Jay helped me out with my gear.

We went to a small compound that belonged to MARSOC, a team which had just arrived from the U.S. and that I was to be working with. Jay gave me a small single room that had a bed and for me that was like the Hilton. But he told me I would only be there for two nights so I made the most of it enjoying my last showers, probably for a while according to what the others kept telling me, and eating my last decent meals. That night I sat on my bed wondering why the heck I didn't quit. But I told myself I had to serve my country, and besides I must do it for my family, a nice house for my wife Rashida and my son Ilyas. But they seemed an awfully long way away.

CHAPTER 7
GOLF COMPANY ON THE LONG ROAD

Someone knocked on my door. I opened it to a tall good looking guy who introduced himself as Rob. Immediately he handed me a phone saying he needed me to translate between himself and an Afghan. It felt good to at last be doing what I was here for but I was also a little nervous and afraid of screwing up. The voice speaking Pashti came through clearly and the message I sent back was simple. Rob thanked me and flashing a big grin, left. I relaxed and felt better about everything.

Later on Jay came back to my room and told me we were going to leave early in the morning so I started packing up and was ready by the time he came back for me at two AM.

I took my duffle bags outside and found myself in the midst of chaos, the yard full of soldiers finding their Humvees and loading their stuff. Jay directed me to my vehicle and put my gear in another. I found out I was to be sitting next to the team captain, Andy. It took a couple of hours before we started leaving the base and headed up to a stretch of our route that Andy told me was extremely dangerous. Last year, he said, a convoy from here on their way to BMG, got ambushed and never made it.

First though, the highway took us through Herat city. Kids came running after us so skinny and big eyed, asking for food and water; I felt terrible but had nothing to give them. The convoy stopped and I heard Andy asking on the radio, "What's going on?"

We heard back that one of our supply trucks had had an accident. Now I had time to look around and saw butcher shops with meat hanging in the open, flies buzzing everywhere, and milk, butter, cheese and eggs being sold uncovered on the streets. Motorcycles were the main means of transportation, a few donkeys and old bicycles. The air smelled of rotting vegetables.

We finally started moving again and as we left the city the paved road became the most shitty dusty road on the planet and, following everyone else's example, I wrapped a scarf around my head to cover as much as possible of my face.

We kept pushing on and came across a small river. The whole convoy came to a stop and we were told that one of our fuel trucks had been flipped into the water due to the local driver being high on something. I saw all the nearby villagers running with buckets, sprinting to the truck to get fuel for themselves. Our team captain Andy was upset and felt bad that we poisoned their only supply of fresh water but the people just seemed happy to get the free gasoline. We pulled the driver out of the truck and threw him into another then, leaving the crashed vehicle behind, the convoy was back on its feet.

We started pushing through rugged mountains and just over the top of the highest, our convoy stopped at a checkpoint of the Afghan National Army. While our guys took a break and dropped off some supplies they had been asking for, I went and talked to the soldiers stationed there. They were hungry for news and I lied to them about how well the war was going and that soon it would probably be over. I knew it wasn't true but at least it lifted the spirits of these guys stuck up on the mountain top with, by the look of it, not much to keep them warm. I learned that some were in the army out of patriotism and some just for the 200 dollars a month pay but most were pretty depressed and stressed out by having to expect a Taliban attack at any minute.

Even though I don't smoke I gave them the packet of American cigarettes I always carried to make friends with and regretted not having the pot they would rather have. As I walked back to my group I wondered if I smelled as bad as those guys had.

We started moving again, going down into a vast valley. Shortly we came to another checkpoint of the Afghan National Police and here we stopped for a few minutes to chat and drop some more supplies. At least they were warmer than their unit on top, and closer to civilization, if you could call it that way out here.

At this point we were getting close to the city of Qal-E-New. We could see city lights and drove past an airport runway on the Spanish base.

Soon we rolled up to a gate a soldier was guarding and he directed us in to where we were to station the convoy and spend the night. We all clambered out of our vehicles and tried to wipe the dust from our faces while stamping our feet in an effort to beat it out of our clothes but it was as though we had rolled in the grey powder and would never get rid of it.

Jay came up to me and said, "Let's go talk to the truck drivers." I spent a while translating the language of Farsi and Pashto into English then out of the corner of my eye I noticed strange activity and stopped in mid-sentence to look. The local truck drivers were stealing our fuel! "Jay, Andy! Look!" I pointed to what was going on.

They both looked then both shrugged. "Don't worry about it we have plenty," Jay said and turned back to the men he was talking to; and I continued translating. It was a different world and I would have to get used to it.

It was late so I pulled out my sleeping bag and tried to find even ground. It was nothing but gravel and my sleep was no better than little sharp stones would allow. The next morning I awoke to hear the truck drivers refusing to drive our trucks to BMG, they said they thought the contract was to only come this far. I jumped up to translate as the problem was quickly becoming heated and I told them they must listen to Lieutenant White because the Army was in charge of their contract. Lieutenant White told them they wouldn't get paid unless they took our stuff to BMG and at that the drivers backed down, but I could hear them grumbling as they climbed back into their rigs.

Later, our convoy on the move again, we drove through a junkyard of planes with kids climbing and playing everywhere among them. *Ilyas would love a chance to do that. I smiled to myself.* We crossed that runway into the city where locals started crowding our vehicle and more and more people filled the streets. We had a growing fear of someone opening fire; anything could happen in a big crowd like this.

We refilled our trucks but now the truckers refused to pay for their gas and we had no choice but to pay for them so we could get out of this fearsome looking crowd.

We started moving again and, finally leaving the town, we rolled up to the Spanish base as night fell. By now wherever my sleeping bag lay was home.

We got the convoy out of the base early next morning and rolled up dangerous stretches of road past small villages. In one I saw a kid sitting on the ground literally eating sheep's poop. I was in shock after I saw that. I never knew Afghanistan had villages like this! As I was passing by I felt such pity that I threw all of my personal energy bars towards the kids and they started running full speed towards the Humvees.

I heard a voice from Ski, our eyes in the sky as we called him as he sat on top of the Humvee as lookout and called in Air support if needed. "Azizi take it easy, you might need them yourself," he yelled. Then I looked at my captain Andy next to me and he was only smiling.

We were pushing through the most dusty, narrow roads and when we pulled up to a small village and saw an old man, we stopped the convoy. Captain Andy said, "Go talk to him." I replied "OK,"and got down onto the dusty ground.

The old man thought we'd brought food and blankets for his village and looked disappointed when I had nothing.

"Are there any Taliban here?" I asked him.

He said, "No." And then asked if he could have boots and blankets for his kids since winter was approaching.

It was heartbreaking to see the suffering of these people so when I got back into my Humvee I found the little cash in my pockets and dug it out to give him but the convoy was already starting to move and he was left behind.

CHAPTER 8
ENEMY CONTACT

We got to a hill so steep that most of our vehicles couldn't make it so we sent a high grade army truck to the summit and used his rope to haul everything up that couldn't make it on its own. Finally the whole convoy was gathered on top after a long noisy afternoon.

We were only a few Kilometers from the Turkmenistan's border and it was already dark when the sky started to fall in pounding rain. Our team found an elevated mound from which to scan the area through their high intensity night vision goggles and I was left sitting next to Andy in the Humvee. A loud thump startled us. Andy jumped out as someone yelled, "Enemy contact!" Our gunner Jamie, operating the 50. Cal, started firing at the invisible enemy and immediately bullets were flying everywhere. I stayed put in the Humvee pissing my pants. I heard people shouting about enemy RPG's going off and when one almost hit one of our fuel trucks, it scared the shit out of everyone.

The enemy had an advantage as they were at the top of a hill looking down on us and as I saw the flash of guns firing I started thinking about my son. "Shit, Im gonna die here!" I thought. Andy was calm asking Ski for Air Support, but it was too cloudy and these were no conditions for any planes to come our way.

We managed to hold our own until finally the rain let up and we heard a plane over head.

The attacking Taliban, realizing we now had backup, disappeared while we, realizing the Afghan Border Police Outpost was only a few kilometers away, rushed everyone into their vehicles and got the convoy moving as fast as we could. I was still in shock, sweating and shaking after my first contact with the enemy.

We made it to the Afghan Border Police outpost with no trouble, and quickly set up a perimeter around the convoy. Sunrise came quickly, and I was kept busy translating between Rob and Pat, two very skilled MARSOC warriors, and the Afghan Border Police, telling them about what we had gone through and where we were heading.

There were only a few police at this outpost with not a lot of ammunition, so I could see that hearing of the Taliban being so close made them nervous. We helped them out by giving some ammo and other supplies we could spare in repayment for their hospitality and I think that made them feel better.

Late in the morning we left the Outpost but before long were stopped by another steep hill. This time it was soon decided to be impossible for our trucks to get up as there was also deep mud to contend with caused by the previous night's downpour. Everyone was on super alert for fear of another ambush so, as we couldn't budge them, we started burning the fuel trucks one-by-one, knowing how much the enemy would have loved all that free gasoline. With explosions and a deafening roar the heat of the flames joined with that of the noonday sun to give us an uncomfortable sample of hell and we were relieved when the last truck was rendered a useless wreck and we could move on.

Finally we reached the vast valley locals called Alkazi , which was not far from our destination, Bela Murghab. (BMG). There was something some might call an intersection, two different roads leading in two different directions, and we saw a truck in the distance on one of them coming towards us. As it drew closer I saw men, at least fifty of them with long beards going down below their bellies. Team Captain Andy called me over, "Azizi come here. Go over and ask them which road leads to BMG."

At this point I gave Andy a look that said, "Are you crazy?" I didn't even have a weapon on me, and no amount of money would make me go down to that truck load of beards.

Andy was quiet a minute then he said, "C'mon, we'll go together."

So we got out of our Humvee and started walking.

As we got closer and it didn't seem to raise any concerns I asked in their native language, "Which way is Bala Murghab?"

Andy had told me before I started to talk to them that he already knew which way BMG was and this was to be a test to see whether they were going to lie or not. So what do you know, they told us to go the opposite way, which would have lead us straight into Taliban territory.

We went back to the convoy, told them to pack it up and then we started to push the correct way towards the town of BMG. In a little distance we rolled through something like a small camp with scattered Hallway longhouses made of mud everywhere. All you could hear was dogs barking through the mud bricked walls and I figured the inhabitants must be hiding from us.

We passed out of this part of the valley and kept moving toward our target town and Forward Operating base (fob) TODD named after a much respected Captain Todd who had been killed there.

CHAPTER 9
FOB TODD

Our convoy, or at least what was left of it, wound through narrow, winding streets of the bustling city of Bala Murghab raising clouds of dust no one seemed to notice. I supposed that having a main base on their perimeter had gotten these citizens used to Army vehicles disrupting their routines. We drove around a last corner and there was FOB TODD in all its glory. It really wasn't different from other bases; maybe a bit more impressive with guard towers standing at each corner and giant walls to protect everyone inside.

The convoy split up once we entered; cargo trucks and GMV's took our supplies to what was designated as our area of the camp while the other vehicles went to their assigned station. I was full of gratitude to our driver Floyd, for getting us safely here as, at times, I'd expected the same fate as the previous convoy which never made it-and me with no dog tags!

I swung out of my Humvee and, looking around, couldn't recognize any faces behind their layers of dust. I removed my body armor, drew in a deep breath of relief, and then joined everyone else in unloading our gear into the two tents provided, each of which couldn't fit more than 6 people. The only floor offered to us was more dust. Night was coming so we got busy putting up more tents with our cot beds in them and, after a snack of the army rations we always carried with us, I know that I collapsed into exhausted sleep.

Morning came abruptly with news that two 82nd airborne soldiers had just drowned in the nearby river. We were told that there had been a previous airdrop of supplies but one package landed in the water and one of the soldiers went in to get it. Evidently he got caught up in something and when a fellow soldier came to pull him out the heavy weight of their gear took them both under. No one could rest until they were found, every division and rank was helping in the search.

The effort continued all my first day there and during the long hours of searching through mud and water I would often hear distant gunfire then moments later see our jets streaking overhead in its direction.

The second day at FOB TODD, I went with Jay to translate at his meeting with the Commander of the Afghan National Army. I started off to walk the long, only way I knew to get there but Jay called me back. "This way," he said jerking his thumb toward a rickety ladder climbing up one wall. I didn't like the look of it at all. It looked slippery and precarious but as Jay was already half way up I had to follow. We dropped down the other side into the Afghan Army portion of the base and then entered a compound where we saw a fatass sitting in a big wooden arm chair watching us approach. This was Colonel Ali. He did not stand as Jay and I introduced ourselves.

"And what did you bring me from the U.S.?" he said.

As I translated this for Jay I had to suppress a grin as he answered, deliberately misunderstanding this quest for gifts, "Good fighting marines, Sir."

The Colonel's face grew dark as he listened to my translation. Then we went on to assure him that we were here to do anything he demanded. "We are here for you," we emphasized.

He said he had a lot of soldiers and we promised to train them.

With that we left their compound and, returning by the long the way to ours, I couldn't help bursting out to Jay with, "And that's the commander of the Afghan forces?!"

"Yeah, and to think, first thing he wanted was a gift! Selfish, lazy bastard. I just hope his men are better."

"And it was so hot in there!" I pulled up my collar and shivered, "He must be the only one on this base with some kind of heater while the rest of us freeze!"

I later found out that the Colonel also had his own comfortable private room in a small mud compound just behind the wall of our own area.

After this troublesome start my day grew brighter when I found that a fellow interpreter from Camp Stone was at FOB TODD so I wasn't the only translator here! Now I had a friend to keep me company.

We had hired some locals to work in the base and make it more livable: put in plumbing, kitchens and divided rooms, and now they arrived. The youngest was five and the oldest seventy. I could see this was going to be a long project. They were to show up every morning and leave at night. I translated between them and MARSOC, introductions and a few minutes to talk, then I went back to my tent, at this point to be available for any team member who needed me to translate anything he needed.

Around noon someone told us they had just found out that there were Italians on the other side of the base so finally we could have a hot meal. I dropped everything and ran over there to grab some food, coming back a short time later feeling much better. Amazing the difference a full belly can make on a man's view of the world!

CHAPTER 10
SEARCH'S END

The search for the two drowned soldiers was still active and while most of our team was over there helping, the rest of us were told to set up a safe zone for the weekly supply drop which was expected within the hour. Men drove Humvees to protect a large perimeter, and when the C17, the biggest army cargo plane we had arrived and I stood watching its load descending safely from the sky, without warning, a swarm of local men and kids pushed past us. They seemed to appear from nowhere, attacking the pallets, each one frantic to get his arms around as many tempting American goods as he could. We did our best to control them but it was like trying to hold back an ocean tide until at last a massive truck with a lift appeared to load and haul the supplies back to base.

Now the villagers wanted the parachutes so, as we didn't need them, we said okay and that was like lighting a firecracker as adults and children, again flung themselves into battle for the silken prizes. I stood amazed at the chaotic scene which, I was told, was repeated with each supply drop.

I didn't have time to see how many bloody noses and bruises were the result of this rampage as I had to get back to the river, pushing aside reeds and deep mud in our search for the bodies of our two fellow marines.

A Taliban town was on the opposite bank so we had to be on constant alert for an attack. All seemed quiet until a couple of mornings later someone reported hearing enemy fire in the distance. I stopped to listen and above the rippling of the current heard gun shots and explosions rapidly coming closer. My shouted warning sent everyone scrambling for the bank and picking up their weapons. The shooting was really close now coming from across the water. Our men returned fire and soon our gunners with the 50 caliber weapons mounted on the tops of their Humvees joined us with ten times the enemies' response. Finally the Taliban fell back.

That brief fire fight hadn't taken long but we'd had to hit them with everything we had before they backed down. Now we went back to base where everyone found a place to rest and clean his rifle.

"Let's go see the Commander of the Afghan National Army," Jack, one of our team said, so I got up and followed him to where Commander Ali dozed in his tent.

I translated for Jack saying how, although we had only started to train his guys, maybe we should discuss taking them on missions with us as we could really do with more fire power.

Commander Ali wasn't too pleased with the idea, saying he was worried about his men. He seemed to hint that a few gifts might make it easier for him to decide and the chocolate bars Jack took from his pocket seemed to help.

I talked back and forth between them until they came to an agreement for us to take some of his soldiers with us next time and, as we left, he told us what kind of American chocolate and cigarettes he liked best.

That night I lay in the warmth of my cold weather sleeping bag, on the ground outside my tent gazing up at the sky. The stars were so close it almost seemed as though I could touch them. The sky was so lit up and beautiful and peaceful it made me wonder why on earth we humans were so intent on fighting each other.

Morning came quickly. We heard the sound of heavy Chinook and Blackhawk helicopters landing on the dusty heli pad. A special Team of Nato Divers had arrived with special forces and army commandos to help with the search. Later on Special Forces went to take out a little Taliban group tucked away on the other side of the river, probably the same ones that had previously attacked us but, Special Forces reported, they had also seen many more of the enemy assembling over there

Our team Dagger 22 and all of our members began grabbing their gear and guns preparing for a big fight. I had a bad feeling that lots of people were going to get injured in this battle.

CHAPTER 11
THE TOUCH OF HELL

Afghan commandos and Army Special Forces went in first and we, the so called Quick Reaction Force, waited. Soon word came that the Afghan commandos were badly outnumbered and getting slaughtered so then they sent us in to help.

We left in our Humvees and crossed the bridge over the river. It was a long mostly straight dusty road that led to the Taliban village and when we reached it everything was deadly quiet. The place looked like a ghost town. Completely empty. Or at least so we thought.

Out of nowhere a man shouted. Immediately Rocket propelled grenades and ak47s came at us. Caught by surprise we didn't exactly know where the heavy enemy fire was coming from. We requested Air support and started shooting back rapidly at random locations of where the Taliban could possibly be. Not being allowed, as an interpreter to carry a weapon, for me it was like I was always caught in the middle of a fire fight completely frustrated at not being able to help my side.

Our jet, called a Hawk, flew by dropping a storm of bullets so rapid it seemed like god was spitting lead. It was so loud that we started laughing, maybe a nervous reaction, as it flew back and forth firing rapidly at the enemy. Then a bomber appeared overhead and dropped one bomb that shook the whole valley. I must have heard at least one million rounds of ammo fired that day as the fight lasted hours, and was indescribably gruesome.

We heard that the interpreter in the team that went first, the ODA, got shot in the face. They tried to bring him back but he died.

A Chinook Helicopter landed a few hundred feet from the firefight to take on injured men. Since I didn't have a gun Andy, using my new nick name, said, "Easy, go help them." So I found myself carrying injured to the Chinook. It was horrifying for me to see men with gaping bullet wounds and blood dripping everywhere. Some suffered other injuries such as losing their legs to Rocket Propelled Grenade explosions and, hearing them moan, I felt desperate and useless at being so unable to help them

It also made me go cold to see the faces of our soldiers still fighting while looking utterly exhausted.

Later, back in base, after what happened and what I experienced I was so depressed and sad that I just slumped down on the ground, shaking and cold, trying not to think at all.

Jack appeared in front of me and said, "Let's go see Commander Ali."

In the Colonel's tent we discussed taking more of his men ASAP on some of our missions. We agreed to train them and he, with a bit of chocolatey encouragement, finally agreed to supply us with soldiers.

We walked back to our quarters as day was coming to an end. Quiet and peaceful it was hard to believe that all the things I had experienced only a few hours before could be other than a bad nightmare.

CHAPTER 12
HEROES AND VILLAINS

The next day I woke up early to attend the meeting held each morning unless we were off on a mission. It was at the district Governor's Building across the river and all the available Commanders of every rank and country were there.

I, as translator, went with Andy and a few others so they could discuss how to make peace in this area, always hoping to come up with a plan on how to make this a better place, but no ideas were ever easy to carry out or at all certain of any success.

After the meeting, we went to the village past the bazaar to check on the damage done by the bomb we dropped yesterday. When I got to the site, which turned out to be just one large bombed out building, I met the head of the BMG Police Department and. pretty much the whole day was spent talking to him and the village people explaining to them how no civilians, only Taliban, had been killed and that keeping the locals safe was our top priority.

We drove back to the fort as daylight faded. Every chance I got, I went to talk to the local employees we had hired to work inside our base and, like the villagers I had been speaking with that afternoon, they all seemed like friendly, decent men. I knew, however, that some of them were surely Taliban but I had no inkling which. The head of the group, an avid Taliban hater, became my trusted informant and for a small monetary recompense told me of any enemy sympathizers he came across and I had to fire them. All these people were poor, and struggling to make a living for their families so I figured they did what anyone would pay them for, which included fighting against us while working for us. It bothered me to have to distrust everyone, from the highest official to the lowliest peasant, but that was the way it was.

Everyday those truck drivers who had brought our supplies from Herat kept asking us for more water and food or a plane to fly them out, so dealing with them was a constant irritation. Poor guys were stuck, living in tents on the edge of the base with no way to get home as they definitely weren't going to drive back through Taliban territory by themselves without us. It turned out to be an unpaid six months before they did finally get a flight home.

By now I was really comfortable with my fellow team members and as we became friends we would talk about our lives and families back home and I would be ready to translate anything here they needed.

The nights were getting colder and I zipped up my sleeping bag and hid myself in it like it was my shell. One night it hit below zero and the next day I was awakened by yells and leapt up not knowing what was going on. Outside my tent was a shocking sight. A British diver had found the body of one of the 82nd drowned soldiers and there was the casket with him in it. It was quickly identified as Ben Sherman, a twenty one year old boy who had risked his life to save his friend.

I later found out that he had a pregnant wife back home whose girl child would never see her father but would grow up knowing he was a real hero. Later that day they covered his casket with an American flag, and we were all there, every rank, even the Bala Murghab District Governor. We said our final words and paid our respects. Then we fired shots into the heavens and later choppers came to take him on the first leg of his journey home.

CHAPTER 13
TRAINING OTHERS, AND UNDERSTANDING THIS AFGHANISTAN

It was very quiet, and early. I was just sitting there on my dusty cot feeling sorry for myself and thinking about my kid and my wife when Jack rushed into my tent. "They are here, and they are ready!"

I followed him outside and saw the Afghan National Army members waiting there ready to be trained. A raggedy lot, tall, short, fat and thin, all young in ill fitting Afghan Army uniforms. They were sent by Commander Ali, fifteen soldiers that were all ours and would be with us completely under our command. I could envision almost every one if my team members assisting with the training, and I would be involved with helping them communicate, translating in Farsi, Pashto and English.

But first we got them any gear they needed, mainly decent boots. We also checked out their weapons as they would immediately start daily target practice. We taught them how to be quiet, how to handle their guns, and soon they would know their Ak47 better than they knew their own beards. We gave them lots of pep talks and taught them how to not to panic in the midst of gunfire.

Our medics, Ryan and Heath, trained their medics how to close wounds and use a tourniquet. This was the most translating I had ever done because most of these men didn't know any English and for that reason it took weeks to get them where they needed to be.

Jack and I would regularly go to Commander Ali's office to tell him how everything was going. First we would give the sloppily dressed, over weight man his "gifts." There was one day when Jay and I were called there to fix a broken radio and took it to the technician tent located nearby. Two men were there working on electrical equipment that if broken down out in the field could mean life or death. I was surprised to see they were both Chinese and Jay was particularly amused, on the way back with our mended radio saying, "So now the Chinese are over here in Afghanistan too!"

Besides us training the Afghan Army I started to get trained too. As a translator I hadn't been allowed to carry a gun so I'd never received the training, but now, after being in the middle of that last fire fight, my friends and superiors said it was time. It was a big boost to my morale to find I was a naturally good marksman and I enjoyed the praise after proving myself best shot on the range.

As a routine we would go out and patrol small villages to befriend the people and gain some underground knowledge. By now we knew the streets and the locals very well, well enough to be informed of people helping the Taliban who I had thought of as staunch allies in our war. It was a shock to realize that here I could no longer trust my own intuition as to who was friend or foe.

There was one day when I was sitting in my tent talking with a friend, when Billy, one of our team operators, burst in pissed off and fierce.

"Billy, what's wrong?" I asked.

"Someone working on this base, a local guy we trusted, is a spy for the Taliban. I know this for a fact."

I knew the man he alluded to; older, although most every mature person native to these parts looked old, he had a friendly toothless smile whenever we met and even said, "Howdy, Pardner," his only English learned from some western movie I presumed. To have been a spy he must have known a lot more than that!

Billy and I wanted to kick this guy's ass but instead everyone agreed to throw him out and ban him from coming back. Which we did immediately much to the old guys apparent bewilderment although several of his fellow workers told me that was put on too.

Late the next day Jay came into my tent and called me by my nickname. He said, "Easy, let's go to the Army side of the base."

We walked over there and entered a tent. I asked Jay, "Whose place is this?"

"Sherman the guy that we pulled out from the river," he answered.

We were here to pack up his belongings and send them back home. There I saw his computer on his desk, his clothes on his bed just the way he left them. I couldn't stop getting choked up when I saw pictures of his wife on his bed and his other belongings beside them. I looked over at Jay where he was packing up the dead boy's clothes and then I started putting his pictures and computer into a bag that would soon be heading back to his family in Massachusetts.

The next morning a villager came and stated that he had found the second body down river. It was the body of Brandon and everyone rushed to the scene to help get him out. Just like Sherman's everyone was there for the memorial; every rank - we were all saddened by this tragic occurrence. The chopper was there to fly him back to Herat, than home, where his family waited. Operation Hero Recovery had come to an end.

The air seemed frozen as I got up, thinking about the previous day's memorial. I tugged on my boots, heaviest pants and jacket, then walked out of my tent. At first glance I saw men cleaning and oiling their guns, Everyone was busy. That meant we must be heading out on a mission.

I rushed back inside to collect everything I might need and emerged to see my teammates already getting into their Humvees and revving their engines. Andy yelled from the one in the front of the pack, "Easy, we don't have all day!"

Jeez, why hadn't anyone told me!

We started rolling as I got into my Humvee, and passed through our gate which the Italians opened for us as they waved goodbye.

I found out we were heading towards the direction of Daneh Pasab and the drive was slow as we headed down a muddy, windy road. The first village we reached was small and quiet with ours being the only way through. There were kids running and playing with a soccer ball as we slowly progressed but no one else until we spotted an elderly man walking on the side of the road. Our team captain, Andy, suggested we stop and talk to him so Rob decided he would go, taking me to translate. We got out of the Humvee onto the muddy, uneven ground and started walking towards the man, our heavy boots thumping to advise him of our approach as he showed no awareness of our presence.

We advanced carefully and I put my right hand on my left chest, nodding while wishing him, "Salaam" and he replied with a similar respectful Muslim greeting. I told him my name and then at Rob's urging to hurry it up asked if there were any Taliban in the area that he knew of.

The old man paused a moment, as his brown eyes searched mine, judging me for understanding, then he said, "I am Taliban when you guys are not around. As long as you have permission from the village elder it's fine to go, without that it's not safe anywhere here for you."

We asked him a few more questions, then thanked him politely, and went back to our Humvee.

We told our team captain, Andy, about what happened and drove on through the rest of the village, seeing no one but feeling watched through the cottage windows. Upon reaching open country I took a deep breath, not having realized I'd been holding it, and looked around. To my right were vast green fields of crops and grass with peacefully grazing cattle and sheep, to the left rolling hills which lead toward great jagged mountains. All so breathtakingly beautiful – but all made ugly by war.

CHAPTER 14
CEMETERY HILL

Even though I was there as interpreter for my team I was also in charge of the Afghan National Army soldiers we had trained; so every now and then I would peek in the rearview mirror to see how they were doing. There they'd be rolling along in their Toyota pickups with guys standing on the bed of the truck with their RPG's. They weren't as well equipped as we were so if anything happened I knew we would have to look out for them.

We were coming to where the road ended at the base of a giant rise we called Cemetery hill. As we got closer the sun went behind a cloud and everything grew strangely still and quiet.

"RPG!" The shouted warning only just preceeded the Rocket Propelled Grenades that began hitting us from every direction. Gunfire crashed around us. I saw Jay and Pat hopping onto the 50. Caliber and rapidly shooting back. The rest of us took cover behind the Humvee from where we returned fire with our M4 rifles. Surrounding us were walls on each side of the road and a few houses. RPG's were hitting us from every corner but we couldn't see exactly where the Taliban were. Again it was like fighting ghosts.

I saw jets maneuvering above us so I knew Ski had already dispatched for Air support and I hoped they'd hurry. The Afghan National Army soldiers were confused as they were still in training mode and at this point we were getting hit from every direction. Though we tried to retaliate no one knew where the enemy was, although they could obviously target us. I had been given an Ak47 before we left on this mission and I now used the scope to scan the village and make sure it was clear of civilians. The rules of war made it very clear that no local noncombatants were to be injured by US forces no matter what the circumstances, which made it very frustrating when the Taliban had no such restrictions-and certainly no moral inhibitions.

Joe decided we shouldn't go any farther so we turned the Humvee around and, with the others behind us, drove away as fast as we could back toward Fobb Todd. It was a good decision Joe and Andy made, as not even our plane could spot where the Taliban were hiding and had we stayed someone was going to die there for sure.

By the time we reached the Fort, which wasn't far, the sky had grown dark and it was good to hear the gates close behind us.

CHAPTER 15
THE BEST OF TIMES

Jay had told me a while ago that I should be patient because there were more interpreters on the way to share my heavy work load and the next day I was informed it was time to go pick them up. Three men arrived in a Chinook helicopter and Jay and I introduced ourselves and drove them back to our side of the base and the small tent we had prepared for them. We chatted on the way and although they all seemed nice Afghan guys I discovered that only one spoke English, which was rather odd for a translator. I would immediately have to get to work teaching the other two and I just hoped they were quick learners.

I liked my hours of training the Colonel's Afghan troops, and my English lessons for the new interpreters, but what I enjoyed most were my frequent visits to the local town's bazaar. We did this to talk to the shopkeepers and elders in order to gain first hand knowledge about the underground movements of the Taliban. I, sometimes with a couple of friends, would stroll through the busy aisles and at first the people were suspicious of us, but soon that disappeared as we would buy things, like blankets, which I took back and gave to the rest of my comrades in camp, for the nights were getting shiveringly cold. Besides talking to the vendors I loved to joke with the many children until soon we became accepted and were met with smiles and handshakes. Seldom did I see a woman among the crowd and if I did she was always covered from head to toe in her black chador. The children, their blue, green and brown eyes showing the history of times this area had been invaded by foreigners, became our great friends, wooed to us at first by the abundant candy bars we gave out and later by games of football and American phrases they enjoyed learning.

Watching them sometimes I thought of my own lucky son with plenty of nutritious food and clean water, good schools, warm clothes and a bright future to look forward to. These children had only bread to eat and no future. Even in the Afghanistan of my childhood, before the Russians came the people were friendly, neighbors helped neighbors, children played with no thought of bombs, everyone went to school and always ate a good meal at the end of the day. What had happened to my country? My wonderful, kind people?

I felt accepted into the villager's lives and in time we all worked together to build a school for the kids and even hired a teacher, his meager salary, a lot for him, was paid for by the American marines in our corp. I almost forgot that some among my village friends might be the enemy.

Then one day, when I was on base, an ANA soldier was killed by a police sergeant due to an argument that broke out in a shop. The name of the police sergeant was Shah Wali and when we raided his house we found he was hiding a ton of explosives and weapons. He was busted and found guilty of helping and working with Taliban. Charged with Murder and Corruption he was sent back to Herat city, tried by the Afghan court and eventually hanged. This was upsetting for me as I had trusted him with never a thought of his being Taliban. Soon after that I discovered the district Governor we met each Monday to discuss plans with, and his chief of police, were also Taliban but we didn't let on, were careful what we said and often used it to our own advantage by spreading wrong information about our movements. I had however learned my lesson, that no one here could be beyond suspicion.

I learned a lot of inside knowledge from talking to bazaar shopkeepers and elders and developed a great respect for these men who struggled to do their best for their families in this desperate war torn area. I hoped our being there could one day get rid of the Taliban who demanded "protection" fees from these already impoverished villagers and my one wish was to remove fear and danger from these good people.

CHAPTER 16
BE A LAMP OR A LIFEBOAT OR A LADDER
TO HELP SOMEONE'S SOUL HEAL

Back in the fort, I had grown more and more wary of our bizarre way to get to the Italian and Army section.

That ladder resting against the Hesco wall was so precarious I expected it to collapse at any minute. It was as though every time a man put his foot on the first rung he was signing a paper that said he could break a bone in his body. There was one close call when I slipped and almost fell that made me so mad I complained to our commander but nothing changed.

There was always so much going on that I hadn't been aware of the number of men committing suicide until I heard yelling, cursing and sobbing coming from a tent not far from mine, I ran to see what was the matter and found one of my soldier friends on the telephone, holding a gun to his temple, tears streaming down his face which was contorted with either grief or rage, I couldn't tell which. I managed, with difficulty, to wrestle the gun away from him and as he sank sobbing onto his cot he brokenly told me he had been speaking to his wife who said she had taken the kids and moved in with another man. "He'll be a good father to them, she says."James punched the matress with his fists unable to continue for a moment. He took a gulping breath. "Says she's sorry just couldn't stand being alone any longer. What the hell does she think I'm doing? Having fun at a holiday Camp?" He made a grab for the gun but I'd put it well out of reach and tried to find words to calm him.

About this time the Fort Doctor appeared. He gave James

something to calm him down and was ready to take him to the hospital. He looked at me. "You're name's Easy, isn't it? I've seen you in the bazaar. Lucky you caught this soldier in time, we've lost quite a few. After mail or a phone call usually. Don't these women understand what they are doing to someone whose only hope in life is to survive and get back to them?" He clicked his tongue, looked down at the ground a moment then gently led the still sobbing soldier away.

I sat a moment on his cot trying not to imagine getting a letter like that from my wife-but of course she would never... I shook my head and joined my buddies in the Italian quarters for Spaghetti which I loved. But for some reason my appetite had vanished.

CHAPTER 17
PATHFINDER HILL

When we got back to the tent next day from walking around the Bazaar my feet were in agony. I had worn heavy army boots that weren't meant for walking so my feet had swollen to a slow throbbing pain. My buddy Jamie, seeing me hobble in, took pity and lent me a second pair of lighter boots that he had, and due to what happened next, that probably saved my life.

The next day I woke up to hear Mark and Pat talking beside my tent and when I went out I saw the ANA soldiers being assembled on one side and on the other my Marine corps men busily cleaning and taking apart their guns and loading their magazines.

I knew then that we were going on a long, serious mission. Jay came up to me and said, "Easy, you and another interpreter are coming with us tonight."

I didn't even ask why or where—just worked all day preparing then, after a good evening meal and a nap, briefly checked on the ANA soldiers to make sure they were ready to get moving and, after checking their guns and gear, I collected everything of mine that I would need and we loaded our Humvees.

We had a new State of the art vehicle coming with us which went by the name M-RAP. It was very high tech, with space for only a few crew members but then had a 50. Cal machine gun on the top which was controlled by a joystick and a monitor on the inside, kind of like a real life video game. I thought how my son would love hearing about it.

It had been a long day of getting ready and we weren't due to leave until two in the morning. I saw men looking badass with night vision goggles, radios and heavy armor. They looked very hardcore.

Luckily this time my fellow team member had an extra pair of night vision goggles to lend me so I probably looked tough too. Maybe I'd get someone to take a photo to send home.

We all got inside our Humvees and started our engines. The rule was to never use lights unless moving so now we switched them on, got into line and started rolling towards the front of the base, and the big screeching gate of FOBB TODD. The Italian army guards waved us goodbye as they let us through and we waved back at them, shouting, "Adios Amigos!"

We had only been driving for a very short while before we came to the bridge that crossed the familiar wide river. Whenever we came up to this my heart dropped as the bridge was only supported by three metal beams and the fragile structure shuddered under our eighteen ton Humvees. We now crossed one at a time, driving as quickly as we could, remembering how the water below had already taken two soldier's lives a few months before.

After we had all arrived safely on the other side we moved back into formation and set off along the narrow rough road. We passed the small District Governor building where we'd had meetings every morning on how to bring peace, and right after that we came upon a small Bazaar empty and deserted. We quickly made our way through it and kept following the dirt road which took us past our first checkpoint; a little hut with a sleeping Afghan Policeman guarding it.

We didn't wake the guy, just kept going until we came to a road known to us as the Bowling Alley. It got its name because it was long and narrow with compound walls on either side. It felt like a trap. As cold as it was outside I was sweating because earlier in November there had been a huge fight on this very spot resulting in lots of casualties.

I was nervous, as I guess we all were, because each one of us knew that every compound here was owned by the Taliban. On edge, we drove forward, ready for anything, and our boys on the monitor kept close watch. Someone from another Humvee radioed us, "Keep your heads up."

We reached an intersection. It was not only the biggest in the area but the most dangerous and it went by the name of Taraz.

Every road went to either another quiet village or it could lead us to hell.

We kept going straight, our destination becoming more and more visible. Rolling hills came into view, each frozen top lit by the December moon. In front of us stood the tallest, called Pathfinder. Someone from another Humvee radioed, "There she is buddy, this is us." We had driven half an hour to get to this final destination. Behind Pathfinder Hill there were two other small hills separated by a ridge on which we parked all of our Humvees and set up a perimeter.

We got out of our vehicles and when I got out of mine it was too dark to see anything. Time to put on my borrowed night vision goggles.

One of our team members, George, started walking with his mine detector, searching for IEDs, and we followed, gradually making our way up the back of the big hill.

At the top some of our guys started digging trenches; a hiding place where we could be tucked in but still have a clear view of things. From the corner of my eye I saw Mark setting up his Badass Sniper Rifle.

I looked past him toward the horizon and saw that night was dying, but it was still as cold as shit.

To my right the ANA soldiers were setting up their positions. Daylight grew on us. Day one. Dead silence. We were all scanning through our binoculars for anything suspicious.

A few short moments and it was morning. We were still in our fighting positions watching the area.

Just like any other fight it started when a bullet sped past our heads, then another and another. In no time they were flying everywhere. I dove into my trench. So did James.

Joe yelled, "Get inside the MRAP!" We both leaped out of the trench and got into the big army truck. Everyone else on our team was now firing back as hard as they could, but this time the Taliban attacked with such force we were completely blindsided.

As we were sitting in the high tech MRAP James scanned the area with its monitor trying to find the Taliban. I looked behind us and saw little missiles flying just a few meters from our parked vehicles. Our teammates on the top of the hill were still firing down in front at the Taliban but now we were being attacked from the rear.

There was a village in front of Pathfinder hill that I knew and now realized was full of Taliban. That's where they were holed up. The only thing we could do was just fire back with all we'd got.

They began shooting at us from the south as well and we requested air support.

It seemed a long time until that B-1 Bomber appeared thousands of feet above us. They dropped a warning bomb on the hillside.

Ammunition was running low. The Taliban had the advantage and it was almost noon with non-stop firing.

We requested a supply truck and they radioed back saying one was on its way.

In a short while First Sergeant Zappala arrived with a truck full of supplies and ammunition. They parked at the back of the hill where chances of getting shot were less, and me and James got out of the MRAP that we were cornered in and ran down to take ammo out and carry it up to the guys.

Mark our sniper handler collected his new sniper rifle, Elvis, from the supply truck, got into position and immediately went to work trying to get an advantageous spot from which to shoot back at the enemy.

An urgent message came that towards the South in the village of Kapeh Baba there was a Combat Outpost Prius that was being guarded by the Italians and was now also under heavy enemy fire. We requested Air Support for them too.

I then saw James and Jay setting up a perimeter with our Humvees and other vehicles to give us more protection. Most of the Taliban bullets were hitting the top of the hill from where our men were firing back but so many of the enemy's were also hitting the hill's side that they looked about to make a big hole.

The B-1 Bomber dropped another bomb against the hillside as a warning. I looked over at Mark and saw him taking the Taliban out one-by-one.

The sun was sinking towards late afternoon. Now the Taliban

found a new way to take us down as a PKM machine gun started shooting rapidly at us. We tried to identify the compound it was firing from and when we did we requested for the B-1 Bomber to drop a bomb on it. The plane turned around, got into position, and dropped a two thousand pound bomb right on target. A dust storm rose blocking visibility and a sharp deafening explosion almost killed my ears.

As our strategy of identifying compounds and taking them out was working we studied maps and scouted with our binoculars searching for more.

Soon we identified three more Taliban compounds and dropped bombs on them. The dust storm that came with each grew bigger, and visibility became less.

The Taliban weren't shooting at us anymore. It became quiet. We saw the sun was low in the sky and the long day was coming to its rest. After those bombs we were free from fire and could relax. The Taliban never fought after dark.

It was almost pitch black and Joe and I climbed inside the MRAP to look through the cameras and monitors, keeping a watch on the area. Suddenly we saw movement and froze, holding our breaths as it came closer and closer. Finally it was close enough and James zoomed in. "It's a coyote!"

I looked at Joe and went limp with relief, then I laughed. "Let's shoot him, he's probably a Taliban spy."

Joe and I were both laughing, then Joe said, "He looks like a spy to me."

We both collapsed in fits of laughter letting go of all that long day's tension.

We didn't end up shooting the helpless guy but instead watched him wander off into the night.

CHAPTER 18
ENDLESS COLD SLEEPLESS NIGHT

Joe commanded me and James to go guard the backside of the hill where some of the last gunfire had come from.

Once we got there we thought we might as well dig more trenches so we picked up shovels and started digging for hours in the dark. It was way past my bedtime but at least the effort kept us warm. We took turns watching for enemies through our night vision goggles and, thank goodness, cold dawn arrived with no attack.

I was so sleepy by now that I was about to fall any second so I yelled to Jay over at the Humvee, "Pass me a Rip It." Rip It was the energy drink troops always had alongside in times of prolonged forced wakefulness. One of these gave enough energy to last hours and I figured this time I needed one.

Jay tossed me the can, which I quickly drank. It reminded me of CocaCola so went down easily. The sky was now fully awake. So was I. Day two began. We saw Sergeant Zappala and his truck coming up the hill for the second time to equip us with more ammunition, water and other goods, such as MRE (meals ready to Eat). Along with those he dropped off Rob and Patty, two of our men who were eager to join the fight and give us reinforcement.

They went straight away up to the smaller hill North of Pathfinder to set up their fighting positions while I helped take ammunition back down.

From a distance I saw Ski looking for batteries for his radio which must have died. After all the ammunition was done with, I walked back up to where I wanted to talk with the ANA soldiers and when I hopped down into a trench where a few held their positions I didn't even need to speak before their expressions told me how bone weary and restless they were.

I was just about to talk to one of them when I heard rapid shooting off to my right. It was Billy shooting his Saw machine gun.

I jumped out of the trench and had just started walking down the hill toward some guys filling sand bags when, halfway there, BOOM! Rocket Propelled Grenades were going off all around me. Then another KA-BOOM hit the side of the hill. The ground shook.

The Taliban now started rapidly hitting us with everything they had. I ran full speed, ducking down, and dove into my fighting position with Jay and James. It took us a little while to start shooting back because of how off guard they caught us.

The Taliban shooter with his PKM Russian machine gun started firing at us from a compound towards the South. Ski and Danny asked for the place to be identified by an overhead plane as we must always confirm that there were no civilians there before we destroyed it.

One of our teammates Mikey, the guy who was always joking and making us laugh, got shot by the PKM shooter and as blood dripped down his face we tried to help. Bandages weren't enough. I thought he was dying but when the blood slowed we saw the bullet had gone through his helmet and skinned the top of his head, not cracked his skull at all. Mikey would be okay! So we turned back to the fight.

Minutes later our plane dropped another bomb on the East Ridge where we confirmed Talilban activity. BOOM! A shock wave rumbled through the valley.

After that bomb drop, for a while it was quiet. Then the PKM shooter started firing at us again.

I was looking around when I saw one of my Afghan soldiers hop out of his trench with an RPG. He sprinted down the hill where he held up his Propelled Grenade and shot it at the compound were the PKM shooter was. The missile he launched took out both the compound and the shooter. "What a brave guy!" we all thought as we watched him run back up the hill carrying his RPG and jump back into his trench.

In the Taliban villages there were irrigation ditches from which the hidden Taliban shot at us, so our plane dropped another bomb, and another, so smoke and dust rose in giant clouds over the whole area. James, Jay and I were chanting, "Hell ya, want to mess with us!" as each bomb fell, our adrenalin rising higher than at a football game.

This day was coming to an end. We'd dropped so many bombs that most of the nearby Taliban villages were destroyed. I still smelled smoke as the sun sank below the horizon and it got colder and colder by the minute.

We would have to stay up through the night so I figured it was time for another Rip It energy drink. It was now pitch black and I went to digging more trenches with Jay and James. My hands were numb as I kept working and, despite the Rip-it my eyes kept closing. Time passed into early morning. No one slept, we just kept working. Thanks to our digging, the trenches were so deep that a person could walk in them without being seen.

Some of our Team Members at the top of Pathfinder Hill found human bones and remains. We knew that this wasn't an Afghan graveyard because they would have flags near their graves. The men who found the bones came to the conclusion that they belonged to a Russian soldier from long ago so it wouldn't matter our disturbing them.

Our Medic Ryan came over to look at Mickey's head. The poor guy was still dizzy and unresponsive and although Andy had called in and tried to evacuate him back to base Mickey was refusing to go— didn't want to leave his combat brothers behind.

Joe and I were talking about it when we heard on the radio that back at base one of the ANA soldiers had opened fire on American soldiers.

We immediately decided to keep a closer eye on our own ANA men although I couldn't help telling myself that ours didn't have that Taliban mentality but were all like the brave ANA soldier who that very afternoon had risked everything for us.

CHAPTER 19
THE ART OF KNOWING IS WHAT TO SEE AND WHAT TO IGNORE

These incidents of ANA soldiers turning against the Americans happened much too often however and I was beginning to learn that in this crazy world I shouldn't trust anyone.

We were scanning the area with our binoculars to look for activity when we spotted a suspicious truck moving towards Pathfinder Hill. We told Mark our sniper, and he looked through his scope, reporting back that it wasn't a military vehicle but definitely something shady. Mark then went ahead and, from a distance, shot out one front tire.

The car started to lose control and came to a stop, the driver hitting the brakes hard enough for the road to create a sand cloud covering the vehicle. We made the call for permission to go over and do a search, then three of us approached slowly with our weapons drawn. A man got out and started walking towards the back of his pickup, No words were said. Our group went closer to take a look at what was in the truck bed.

The man pulled out a small girl dripping with blood and filthy, covered with dirt. He then revealed an adult woman who was also filthy with blood stains all over. They both looked dead. The man then started saying in his native language, "You see what your damn bombs did!"

I translated. It turned out that it was a mother and child. Andy, James and I just stood there feeling terrible and filled with guilt to think we had done that. To be sure we all looked closer and saw that each body had been shot in the head with a single bullet. We asked the man what kind of relationship he had with the woman and child and he said, "I'm the Husband and Father."

We got permission from the District Governor to cross this road and take these people back to base. It was clear to us the man had shot the woman and girl in the head and was blaming us as a ruse to get away. He was probably one of the Taliban who had been shooting at us for the past few days. But we said nothing.

The man changed his tire with a spare he had and then dumped the bodies back into the truck. We then gave him clearance to drive towards our base where he expected to get compensation for the death of "his family."

(We later got word that the bodies, after being examined, were found to have been shot from close range. After questioning the man for a while they decided to release him with no negotiation and he then dispersed into the mist of villages.)

After the man and his gruesome passengers left us Andy ordered some ANA soldiers to walk down and into the nearby Taliban village of Kappe Baba. They were sent strictly to search the bomb site and check for any Taliban or Civilians and I went with them.

We saw trails of blood all over the village walkways, but couldn't find any weapons. Instead we found, in the wreckage of collapsed buildings, a scared little puppy covered in dust. We sure weren't about to leave him there and when we'd made it back, carrying the little guy, the rest of the members all fell in love with him. The puppy looked so much like a bear George suggested we name him that. "Bear, it is!" the rest of the group shouted.

The ANA soldiers wanted the puppy because they'd spotted him first. But as much as we thanked them for finding him, there was no way we were going to give Bear to them. George loved that pup and now spent every free moment with him, giving him water, food and playing tug and ball. I think the pup loved him too and it was good to watch them.

I saw Mark still on top of the Hill looking around through his scope. He spotted Taliban in the distance firing at the Prius Combat Outpost which was guarded by the Italian Army soldiers. Too distant for us to help them. It was getting late in the day.

First Sergeant Zappala showed up again with the daily supplies and broke the news of another shooting back at base: an ANA soldier had shot Staff Sergeant Spino, a medic, who they expected would die and was only working there voluntarily from Herat. Zappala also told us the shooter got shot in the foot by an Army guy then tackled by a few men who sat him down and questioned him. He claimed that if he didn't do it the Taliban was going to kill his family. But he was high on Opium so who knew the truth.

With all of us still shocked, Sergeant Zappala left with his men, driving off into the fog. It was almost dark. Once again temperatures dropped. James and I shivered behind the 50. Cal on the Humvee and I was so bone tired due to this being my fourth night of no sleep I said to James, "I'm gonna take a nap." He replied, "Go for it."

I got out of the Humvee, grabbed my half frozen sleeping bag and walked to the trench where I threw my bag down along the bottom and slowly climbed in. I zipped up and just lay there thinking and praying for Staff Sergeant Pino. Then around and around in my head went the mystery of who actually killed that poor mother and daughter. Finally I slept.

NOOO! I quickly awoke jolting upright, awakened by my own yell. I'd had a nightmare that the whole place was getting shot up. I was shaking from not only the nightmare but from the unforgiving cold. I struggled to climb out of my hole. When I finally made it I saw James and Jay still there guarding the area with their night vision. I thought to myself what tough guys they were, after four days of no sleep still staunchly protecting their post.

The foggy, cold morning hit us very early. James and I sat on the ground having an MRE and sipping down a Rip It. We heard nothing, neither gunshots nor movement. It was quiet and peaceful. Had we defeated the Taliban? Joe ordered some men to walk to the east hills and check out the damage from our previous bomb so I joined them. Almost one mile later we made it to our destination.

All we saw were blood trails and we knew it was the Taliban carrying out their dead. No one was there; just a big dent in the hill, debris and blood.

We started walking back to Pathfinder Hill. It was early in the afternoon and, in contrast to earlier, now the sun was blazing. We were all sweating and completely worn out.

We had almost reached our camp, when we saw a line of trucks driving up the hill towards us. When they finally reached the top a lot of people got out and I recognized Colonel Ali, Colonel Nordeen and the new District Governor. They had all come to congratulate us. I also saw that Colonel Bruno of the Italian army and the 82nd Airborne's platoon leader Lieutenant Robinson were there. First they shook our hands and talked to us about our bravery on the battlefield. Then they all went to the summit of Pathfinder Hill to check out our fighting positions. They raised the Afghan flag there and established a Combat Outpost. We talked for a little while then they got back into their trucks and we waved them goodbye.

This was our fifth and final night there, the temperature was dropping and we were dead weary. I had thought we were going to leave that day and I was pissed off that we had to stay another night. I got into my sleeping bag and slept.

The next morning they declared the Italian and Afghan Army would permanently inhabit the new combat outpost and this meant the Taliban could no longer use those intersections for drug trafficking. We packed up our gear and got into our Humvees. Just before we left, the Italian Army arrived with plywood to build a little hut or COP.

We moved out, starting a dust storm that whirled around us. I looked in the rear view mirror at Pathfinder Hill growing farther and farther away and thought about how stressful it all was and how seeing what some of these men had gone through was humbling and something I could never before have imagined. We drove through a small Bazaar, and up over the bridge that we had driven over five days before. The walls of FOBB TODD grew bigger and closer. The gates slowly opened for us and we waved to the Afghan and Italian guards as we drove through and on to our side of the base. .

We all got out of our Humvees and trucks, smiling and just happy to be alive. We hugged and thanked each other, then collected our gear. Finally it felt amazingly good to take off my body armor and kevlar. We were all covered in layers of dust and when I grabbed a bottle of water from my bag and tried washing my face, everyone laughed as it turned to mud. Soon we took all our belongings to our tents, and it was like coming home as I got into mine and flopped down on my cot.

Two hours later I was awakened by the sound of a Blackhawk helicopter overhead. It was noon and I walked to my friends' tents to see if they were up and, like me, craving a good hot meal. We decided to go to the Italian side of the base for spaghetti so we went up the ladder and over the wall.

We had to wait in a long line when we got to the Chow hall but finally I loaded a huge plate with spaghetti and bread. We sat at a table and scarcely spoke a word as each plate got cleaned off very fast and we got up for refills.

After we had walked back to the ladder and climbed over to our side of the base my friends decided to get some rest. I went to check on my ANA soldiers. When I opened their tent most of them were sleeping, only a few awake, and every one of them looked just as beat up as we were.

CHAPTER 20
LET THE ROCKETS FLY

Back in my tent I lay down and was slowly fading away when, BOOM! My whole world shook and rattled. I scrambled outside to find everyone else already there. Evidently a Taliban rocket had been launched at us but blew up just outside the base.

Someone yelled, "In coming!" and I dove back into my tent and yanked on my body armor. BOOM! Another rocket landed just short. Minutes later a third one. We quickly identified them as coming from the south, near the city of Daneh Pasab. Ski grabbed his drone from his tent; it had a camera that we viewed from a monitor attached to the controller. He quickly got it to fly to the exact location from where the rockets were coming.

Once they saw our drone the enemy was smart enough to move to another position so nothing more came at us and all was quiet for the rest of the day but we couldn't relax until night came pitch black and below zero.

Hatch, our team's photographer, and I made a bonfire near our tents to keep us warm and as we sat near the flames we discussed Afghan culture and the country. He started to show me some pictures he'd taken of the beautiful scenery and soon Mickey and Russo joined us. Then before we knew it more and more men had gathered around the fire. I kept talking to the guys near me and everyone was so cool and welcoming I was glad to be around and working with them.

A few minutes later someone put meat on the grill and barbecued, making enough for us all to eat and enjoy. My eyes began to zone out, time to say good night. I walked back to my tent and as I looked up at the night sky and saw the big bright stars that I could almost touch and the milky way floating right over me, I was for that moment wonderfully happy.

"Incoming"! I awoke with a jolt gasping for air, BOOM! Another rocket had been launched at us. I rushed to get into my gear then looked outside. It seemed as if no rockets had hit inside the base... yet. I looked up at the sky and there was another coming straight at us, closer and closer. I held my breath. BOOM! Our world shuddered. Maybe that one hit the Army side. I asked someone and he said, "Yes, it's bad," I later found out that it took the life of one Army soldier and injured others.

This bombardment continued for two weeks. Then it suddenly stopped. I figured they probably ran out of rockets.

Bored I decided to go talk to local employees inside the base who had been asked to help Billy and Jamie who had started building a living space for the next teams. I was talking to the men when I saw King our intel guy walking towards me.

"Let's go to the ANA side of the base to talk with their intelligence guy," he said.

While we were walking King told me that we were only going there to get information so after we'd introduced ourselves we sat down in a private area to talk quietly.

We basically tried to cover a little bit of every subject. and after our little meeting was over we took off and walked back to our side.

"I got to go run some stuff, I guess I'll see you around,"King said.

"Yeah, sure," I watched him walk away, wondering what he was looking for.

When I got to my tent Jack and Pat were there waiting to ask if I wanted to come train ANA soldiers with them. I accepted, thinking they'd definately need me due to almost none of those guys speaking English so we all drove out to an area used for target practice behind a hill right next to base. Once there we set up some targets for the ANA to aim at and after a short briefing they started firing. Jack, Pat and I observed them and gave pointers.

After a while Pat came up to me and said "Have you ever shot anything like this before?" He was pointing at a Mark fifty-seven machine gun that was mounted on the Humvee. It was known for shooting almost one hundred rounds a second.

I replied, "Hell no, that thing's a beast."

"Let's change that and have some fun," Pat was already climbing onto the Humvee and loading bullets into the weapon. He said "What are you waiting for Azizi?"

I climbed up beside him and listened intently as he told me a bit about it and how to use it. Then I was so excited I went ahead and pushed the button. Vibrations ricochet up my arms and I was being shoved violently back and forth. After one or two seconds I realized my finger was still on the trigger and snatched it off.

Pat from a distance said, "Take It easy, Easy." He was laughing.

I realized I'd probably shot four hundred rounds in those few seconds.

There was a steep hill to the west of FOB TODD, and on top was an ANA Combat Outpost (COP) so after we had done training we went up there to see if the ANA Soldiers needed anything. Their squad leader, nicknamed Fonz, was a good friend of mine, so after spending a long time talking, then checking their weapons for needed repairs, we were pretty tired when we started walking back to base.

It was dark and cold and I was about to crawl into my sleeping bag when I saw Jack approaching. "Put on your boots, we are going to the Alkozai school," he said. "We have to make an arrest."

I knew there was a squad of ANA soldiers stationed there. Apparently we had intercepted one soldier's phone and caught him talking to the same Taliban that was launching rockets at our base. Evidently it was he who was giving the locations of where to aim. We rushed to the Humvees and rolled out of the base heading North.

I found myself back on the familiar dusty winding road. Once we got close to the school we were told to be on the look out for any suspicious activity but we arrived peacefully and inside, the ANA Squad leader pointed out the guilty ANA soldier and we surprised him by tackling him to the ground and zip-tying his hands behind his back. We then escorted him into the Humvee, and drove him back to base.

We locked the traitor in a miserable, cold little cell under the bunker as we only kept him overnight and in the morning gave him to the Army because it was their men the rockets were killing and injuring.

CHAPTER 21
WHEN IGNORANCE IS BLISS

Everyone had gotten up early and from the look of it we were going for a long walk. Jack and I went to the ANA tent to inform them we were leaving in one hour. As was normal we didn't tell the ANA soldiers where we were going, in fact even we interpreters didn't know.

By reading the clues of everyone checking their weapons, and getting extra ammunition I figured it was going to be pretty big whatever it was. Andy and Joe gave a last briefing to all of Dagger 22, then we got into formation and left FOB TODD, one by one, this time on foot marching towards the old bridge.

Once across it we headed straight toward the bazaar, then changed our course to go south alongside the river. This was familiar territory as Rob and I would often stop in Khasadar and chat with the villagers. If any looked suspicious we would tell our ANA soldiers to search them, all this secretly so we remained the good guys.

I remembered the last time I was there. I'd been admiring some fabrics for sale in a booth when I noticed one of the younger children in the group who had become our friends. He reminded me of my son and was always so sad and hungry I wished I had more than chocolate bars to give him. This time he hadn't seen me as I watched him advance toward the booth selling racks of freshly baked bread. His hand dove into his pocket and came out with a coin which he slapped down on the counter. The vendor, a savage looking old man, picked up the coin, replaced it with a loaf of bread, then replaced the coin and slid it back to the child who, with a smile I had never before seen, picked it up, replaced it carefully in his pocket, and walked off hungrily gnawing on the fresh loaf.

When he was well out of sight I went over to the bread seller and asked, "What just happened? You give away your bread?"

The old man had a fierce looking nose over which his eyes flashed at me. "No, I give nothing for free. Every day that child buys bread from me. For a long time he watched people buying things. People handing over money and getting change back. But the boy doesn't understand change; to him it was the same money being returned with the purchase. I don't know where he found that first coin but he spends it on bread from me every day. Probably his only meal and I can spare it."

I bought a loaf from him and think he charged me twice the going price, maybe more. Did he wink behind his formidable beard?

Now as we walked on I thought that I must talk to the school teacher about teaching money to the kids. But no, I quickly changed my mind, better leave things as they were.

I smiled to myself but that quickly froze as gunshots cracked our eardrums, I fell to the ground trying to disguise myself with the dirt while everyone quickly got into their positions to fire back.

CHAPTER 22
LIFE IS A BALANCE BETWEEN HOLDING ON AND LETTING GO

We were being attacked by a Taliban PKM shooter who had spotted us from the village of Qabchaq; so now we split into two groups, each with its own ANA soldier and interpreter. I, as always, stayed with our leader Captain Andy and Ski as we started to push deep into the village while the others climbed to high ground on order to keep watch with their high tech binoculars. Bullets whizzed past me. Another enemy sniper began shooting from the village of Daneh Pasab across the river.

I knew that Ski had already dispatched for air support but in some cases, like this, it was hard to get approval. We kept shooting back but the Taliban knew how to hide and how to escape, and they knew the streets better than we did.

It was already afternoon and I was sweating and dehydrated. We started to clear out some compounds looking for an enemy occupied house but they were all empty.

Taliban had used these same compounds when they fought us at Pathfinder Hill, and now we found lots of empty shells on the floor but no weapons. We were still engaged in the firefight and although we spotted where the bullets were coming from, our people continued to deny us a bomb drop. This was one of those frustrating days. It's very hard to fight like this.

So we packed up and headed back east. It was almost dark, there was no plan for us to stay the night and it was raining so we joined up with the other group and walked back to the FOB. Everyone was so dog tired from walking all day that some of the men were falling down on the slippery rain soaked ground.

I was happy to be back in base alive just before nightfall which hit us faster than a Taliban would hit puberty.

Too weary to climb the laddder over the wall to get a square meal we all, instead, each gobbled an MRE then went into our tents and passed out.

It seemed no time until I was awakened by the sound of distant gunfire. I forced myself out of my cot and glanced at my watch: Six, another day.

We were going to the Village of Ludina located north of the bazaar. Captain Perry and his men along with some ANA Soldiers were guarding a small outpost there and we were going to check up on them.

We got into our Humvees and back on the small dirt road heading North.

We had just entered the Village of Ludina and I was already out talking to some locals. BOOM! Startled I ran toward the sound. and found that Foxx and Armstrong, while patrolling, had stepped on an IED. Ski requested our DUSTOFF Chopper team which arrived immediately and airlifted them back to base. We later found out that Foxx had been killed and Armstrong was being airlifted to Herat then to Germany, to be treated for severe injuries.

I know it's war and people get killed in wars, but for me it was always traumatic when someone very much alive was so suddenly and brutally gone. We were brothers, looking out for each other, and I always felt I should have been able to save the victim even though I knew it was impossible

We immediately headed back to base trying to avoid other possible IED's. Rumors sped that some local went to that same exact area and ran over an IED with his Toyota pickup truck. He also was brought back to base with severe injuries.

We all well knew that this was the work of Mullah Muslim, the midget, the Taliban IED maker and a trusted member of Mullah Jailan's Inner circle. The next day a Specialist Matthew Huston and

Josiah Crumpler were Guarding a COP Corvette when the same suspected Taliban PKM shooter sprayed bullets toward them. Both got shot in the head, Our DUSTOFF team arrived and rushed them back to base but they both died.

Three of our men killed in one week. So heartbreaking. I could leave anytime and not risk making my son fatherless and my wife a widow. But I knew my job was important and these were my buddies who depended on me. No way could I quit.

I spent countless hours with the team on many missions. We continued to train 2/1 Kandak and 1/1 Kandak chain of command for the Afghan National Army. I was the lead interpreter on the team and always made sure other interpreter's abilities were up to par.

I am proud and honored to have had the chance to work with the men of Dagger 22. I am proud of their selfless service to our country and for trying to bring peace to Afghanistan. I will always love them like my brothers for being so cool to me and treating me with respect. I am also dearly sorry for our losses in the battle field.

My company Mission Essential Personnel rules that every 6 months we are allowed to take two weeks off. I mentioned to Jay last time we came back to BMG, that my time was coming to an end but it was still a surprise when one morning he came up to me and said, "Easy, there's a Chinook coming for you." I packed up all my duffel bags and said good bye to everyone. Rob, Pat and Jack came last to give me a hug and wish me good luck. Jay helped carry my gear. Me and a couple of more team members headed to the landing zone.

Shortly a loud Chinook touched down with a couple of Black Hawks and we climbed on board. Everything was so quick it seemed like a dream. I loved when the Chinook took off, causing a dust storm underneath us, hiding our fort below. We were still in danger from attack by Taliban as many times they shot at our choppers, but soon we were over the steep mountains of Afghanistan and less than one hour later we had our first stop in the city of Qalenow. As we took on more fuel and a few more guys I remembered last time I was here with our convoy on the way to BMG. It seemed like years ago and me so green and innocent. We took off again bound for Herat city. Looking down on the passing vast landscape of Afghanistan was actually a little sad for me, taking me way back to when I was a child.

Just about thirty minutes later we landed in Herat.

CHAPTER 23
THE LONG WAY OUT

I got my duffle bags and headed straight to the interpreter's tent that was set up waiting for me. Inside I saw Khaleqi and a couple of other interpreters that I knew, but instead of welcoming me everyone just stared. It took a moment for me to realize they were seeing a cave man. My beard was down to my legs and my chest was a bird's nest. I probably stank too. No one recognized me until I said, "Guys it's me, Azizi." Everyone shouted their surprise and Khaleqi said, "Azizi you haven't taken a shower for five months!"

After he said that I felt embarrassed and rushed to get washed up in the very nice showers they had there. I even cut off my long beard and shaved. It felt amazingly good to be clean! And it was a shock to look in the mirror and see the "old" me there.

Next I headed to the chow hall with a couple of guys to grab some food and all the while I was thinking how strange it was to be here, so suddenly back in civilization. While eating I looked around and thought how lucky these interpreters were to be stationed in Herat, this place was like heaven compared to BMG.

The next morning I went to the MEP office to report my presence and the managers gave me an appreciation letter and longevity award. Also a medal for my bravery in combat and in supporting the MARSOC team. Mission Essential Personnal managers here in Camp Stone were good people and very professional. They also helped me out with booking the travel tickets for my Paid Time Off.

The next day I joined the convoy to Herat airport to catch a C130 Flight to Bagram air field where we waited in the terminal for roll call. We retrieved our military cards, collected our duffel bags, then a van drove me around the base to the big interpreter's transit tent that stank something awful. Luckily I got myself a lower bunk, although the sound of jets taking off all night didn't allow for much sleep.

In the morning an MEP manager came for a briefing, after which I took all my duffle bags to the MEP office where I had to leave everything in storage until I came back from my sixteen day vacation.

I went with a couple of other interpreters around the bazaar to kill some time and I must have seen troops from twenty different countries: it seemed as if thousands of troops were stationed there. After a few hours we took a bus back to our tent.

That night it was again hard to fall asleep because of the noise of jets taking off and landing so I awoke early next morning to catch my flight, this time on a civilian plane to our first stop Kandahar, then onward to Dubai where we spent that night .

The next day we took the taxi back to the airport to catch my flight to Frankfurt Germany where I was going to meet my wife Rashida and my son Ilyas.

CHAPTER 24
TRANSITION

There's something about being in an airplane that isolates me from the world and with all the landings and take offs, always surrounded by military personnel, I had almost forgotten the purpose of my trip but now it rushed in on me. For two weeks I was about to return to civilian life. I would be attending the wedding of my sister in law Narges where I would see a lot of family members and as I waited in the terminal I wondered what I was going to say to everybody, I seemed to have been gone for so long.

The airport intercom finally announced that my flight was boarding and I was one of the last ones to be seated.

This was a real jumbo Jet with civilian passengers nicely dressed, and polite attendants who served drinks and, later, food, with a smile. I thanked god I had showered and put on clean clothes! I tried to watch a few movies but could only think of meeting my wife and son.

Six hours later we landed in Frankfurt. I headed straight for the baggage claim, following arrows due to my lack of speaking German: I passed the strict German security and finally arrived at the baggage carousel where my bag was the first one to come out.

I was nervous. I put my coat on and headed for the exit. The sliding doors opened automatically, and there I finally saw my beautiful wife Rashida! We ran to each other and for a moment were lost in a big, wonderful hug while I couldn't stop saying how much I'd missed her. I turned to my sister in-law, Wahida, and gave her a kiss on the cheek then I picked up my luggage and we walked to their car. On the way they asked me questions about how my flight was but there wasn't time to say much as we were in a rush because my youngest sister in-law, Narges, was getting engaged that day, which was cause for a big party. This was also why my son hadn't come to meet me because he was getting ready. My parents had also flown in from the States a few days prior.

We drove to their house twenty minutes away in the smaller city of Bad-homburg. The car pulled up to their door and when I went to the trunk to get my luggage I heard a little boy yelling, "Daddy"! I looked up and through tears saw my cute six year old son Ilyas running toward me. He flung himself at me and gave me a huge hug, squealing with delight as I lifted him high in my arms. We couldn't stop saying how much we'd missed each other and, holding hands, went inside to meet my new Brother in-law Andy for the first time. I also saw Narges my sister in-law and many more family members waiting to hug me but there was not much time to spare so I was rushed through, enveloped in perfumes and fine fabrics. It was all rather bewildering and finally I opened my suitcase, got my suit out and rushed into the bathroom to change. As I looked in the mirror at my clean shaven face and neatly trimmed hair I hardly recognized myself and for a moment, thinking of my buddies still back at Fort Todd, I felt a touch of shame at having left them there.

"Ahmed, time to go," my wife was calling.

The engagement ceremony was held at an historic park in the middle of Bad-Homburg. We drove there in a rush, struggled to find parking, then walked quickly to the reserved location.

Once there I met lots of other close family members. We all stood in our spots and moments later the to be engaged couple walked up a high staircase where they signed the papers,

We all cheered and clapped, then got together for a picture before we left for the Italian restaurant called Restaurante De Guido. I'd heard it was a place that my brother in-law Andy loved and it was wonderful but I was not happy as I could not help comparing all this affluence to the impoverished people I had been living among. No one seemed in the least interested in my time in Afghanistan and I longed to tell them of the starving shoeless children and the women hidden beneath their tents of material.

The food was great and I'm sure everybody enjoyed it. Of course anything was delicious to me after what I'd been eating recently.

After some time of talking and eating we headed back to the house where they talked more about everyday things. As I listened I wondered if they even knew about the war being waged in Afghanistan and how other people were suffering. It was as if no one even noticed I had been away and I felt a little left out and sad even though I told myself I should be happy with all my family around me.

Azizi and General Petraeus

Azizi and General Miller

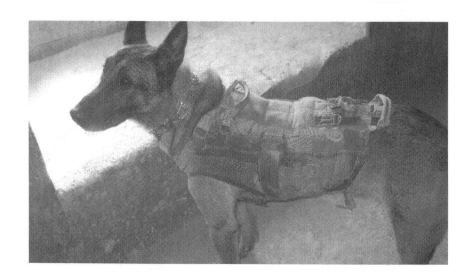

CHAPTER 25
WHICH WORLD IS REALITY?

The next day, after a luxurious shower and shave, my son and I decided to go to a nearby waterpark. We had a great time and while we rested on a bench I told Ilyias about the hungry boys I knew in Afghanistan who had no toys and hardly enough clothes to keep them warm in winter. He looked sad and asked questions as I tried to explain war so he could understand the stupidity of adults. I filled with love for my little boy who seemed sometimes wiser than the adults around him and, wanting to chase away his sadness, suggested we go to the wonderful ice-cream shop not far away.

My sister in-law, Narges, had told me that the wedding was in a week so for most of the intervening days Rashida and her sister went shopping for the big occasion. I seemed to spend most of my time waiting for them, either in stores or at home where they opened and exclaimed over their purchases of jewelry, make-up or clothes.

The day of the wedding arrived, I put on my suit then waited for everyone else to finish dressing. I also waited for Rashida and Narges to come back from the hair stylist in the city. Finally all of us left except for Andy and Narges who came later in a sleek limousine. We got to the wedding venue and there were already hundreds of people there. It was very beautiful like in a movie, with a red carpet that led into the building and later on fireworks in the shape of a heart. We ate great amounts of Afghan food and danced to Afghan music. It was the old times of Afghanistan brought back to life and I thought surely I must be dreaming.

We spent a long time saying goodbye to everyone. My son Ilyas went to a sleepover at his other cousins' house, then the rest of us headed back home to Bad-Homburg.

"I told Ilyas to be ready for us to pick him up on our way to the airport tomorrow," Rashida said snuggling against me in the car. "I've bought him the smartest little new suitcase and wait till you see my new cocktail dress!"

"What airport? I don't have to leave until next week!" I said, startled.

"Oh, didn't I tell you Andy and Narges are honey mooning at a gorgeous resort in Egypt and we're going with them. I'm so excited and you'll love swimming and just loafing in the sun."

"Isn't it terribly expensive?"

"Oh, Andy and Narges are paying for themselves. You'll just pay for the three of us-and, of course, Mother."

"Your Mother is coming too?" I was not too fond of my still gorgeously flamboyant, widowed mother- in- law who led my wife on many of her extravagant shopping excursions. But I did love to see Rashida happy so said nothing more.

All went as planned although I sweat buckets as the Egyptian customs inspected my papers. Egypt and Afghanistan were deadly enemies and of all countries this was the last I wanted to enter.

But here I was and while the women giggled and showed off their figures and jewelry I taught Ilyas to swim and took him to ride a camel, ate huge meals served by clumsy waiters and drank cold beer by the pool.

Four days later we flew back to Germany and I relished the final few days before my leave was up and I must head back to Hell. I tried to make the most of each moment with my family but always this big cloud was hanging over my head.

However much I wished for time to stand still it flew and here I was saying goodbye to all my relatives who waved from their doorway as I got into the car with Rashida and Ilyas. We headed to the Airport where Rashida pulled over to drop me off at the international terminal One. I got out with my bag, hurrying because an official kept urging us to move on as other cars were waiting, so I leaned in, hugged Rashida goodbye and then Ilyas. I started to walk away but shouting stopped me. I looked back and saw the car door swinging open. Illyas jumped out. His mother was screaming at him to come back but my son ran until he reached me. He was holding out something he held in his hands and I recognized his two favorite toys, the white unicorn and Fuzzy Bear. "For the sad little boys," he said in his high child's voice, brown eyes earnestly looking into mine. His mother had reached us and was scolding him as she pulled him away and back to the car.

I watched them drive off feeling my heart die in my chest.

CHAPTER 26
RETURN TO WHERE?

I passed security and got to my gate, then moments later they announced boarding and soon I was back in the air, immersed in the roar of engines, hushed chatter and smells exactly the same as nine days before. Then, though, I had been excited about where I was going and meeting my loved ones. Now I had no notion of where I might ultimately be sent. I hoped for Herat or perhaps even Kabul which would be heaven compared to Forward Operating Base Todd. I slept.

Seven hours later we landed in Dubai, where I found a hotel in which to spend the night, then early next morning I took the two hour flight to Bagram where I collected my duffle bags. No longer was I travelling among civilian tourists and passengers, now I was back among military personnel.

As soon as I could I reported in at the MEP office hoping they would give me my new, hopefully safer, assignment. But all I learned was that I was on schedule to go back to Herat.

In the morning Movement guys awoke me at 3:00AM so I got all my gear together and threw it into the back of a van which took me, and a bunch of other guys, back around the base to the main terminal.

We walked in formation to the bus that drove us to the giant C130, which only twenty minutes later deposited us at Kabul international airport—our first stop. We waited there for a few hours and then got back on the plane and two hours later landed in Herat airport. Here the Spanish were in charge of security and ushered us into the terminal. I felt like a package mailed long distance, being shuffled from one mailbag to another. I think we were all in a zombie state and hardly spoke to one another.

There was a convoy waiting and when I got into my assigned vehicle and started to roll it was like déjà vu once again driving along that infamous Afghan Highway One. In ten minutes we reached Camp Stone.

I was so dog tired I got all my three duffle bags and headed straight to my tent. I never got used to carrying all that heavy gear and after my few weeks vacation it seemed heavier than ever.

Next morning I went to the MEP office to report in and request a rotation, hoping to stay in Herat, but instead they gave me a ride to the Special Force's portion of the base. I went straight to the interpreter's tent and my spirits lifted when I saw a couple of friends. One interpreter was just from the BMG my old station: he give me a hug and then told me that my friend Rob had recently been killed.

It was like a punch in the stomach, Rob was like my brother; we had a special bond. I sank into depression and couldn't really process it. I thought back to the first time Jay came looking for me- and all of a sudden there he was! I couldn't believe it! He gave me a hug then handed me three awards that were sent by Andy our team captain and Joe our team chief. Each wrote me a recommendation letter. The team also gave me an Award of Completion. Jay told me he was leaving to go back to the States and so was the rest of my first team. If I went back to my old base there would be none of my friends there. I felt as though the bottom had fallen out of my world.

The next day I woke up sick, was throwing up and had bad diarrhea. I thought I had a horrible disease and was surely going to die. I went to the medic tent where they prescribed a medication and said I must have eaten something bad. I couldn't even remember eating the day before with all the stops and starts. My wife and son in Germany were like a dream and sometimes I feared that's all they were. And Rob was dead. I wished that was a dream too.

After a week I felt better and was relaxing in the sun when a Special Forces member who was in charge of interpreters came up to me. "Get ready you are going back to BMG."

Oh no! My heart sank. If my old group were still there I might feel differently but I had never yet refused an assignment so quickly went to see the MEP manager on the army side of the base and asked him for my Dog tag. Everyone had gotten a dog tag before, except me, but now I knew how important it was, especially when working in a combat zone, but they still refused to give me one.

The next day I ran into my blue eyed friend Safi, whom I knew from way back in our childhood. He was still working with Special Forces in another part of Afghanistan and we swapped stories as he helped me carry my gear to the helicopter landing zone where I was to catch my ride to Bala Murghab valley where my second team was waiting. The chopper was already there although I spent a couple of hours standing around in the familiar Afghan dust before I finally got on board.

I had cheered up while talking to Safi but now as I looked down, leaving Herat again, I became sad and depressed thinking about Rob and all the other service members who had been killed in the BMG and the fact that I was going back there for the Taliban to have another shot at me. I guess the second team needed me because I had already forged a good relationship with the locals. Made sense whether I liked it or not.

CHAPTER 27
HOTEL COMPANY

We were flying over the big mountain called the Sabzak pass and after two hours I could see the familiar valley where we landed safely at BMG. Bobby, the man in charge of interpreters was there to help me out with my gear and take me to meet the Hotel Company guys, the name my new team gave themselves, and who I'd be working with. This time I was staying in the same tent as Captain Dave, six foot six, in great shape, and team chief Mo, older with a mustache and friendly grin. My fellow interpreters were happy to see me and as soon as the local employees who worked in the base saw me they ran to hug and greet me. All of a sudden I didn't feel as bad about being there! They proudly showed all the hard work they had done while I'd been gone, like digging a well and installing showers in a trailer. But most wonderful was that there was now a door in the wall where the ladder had been. The base was actually starting to look like decent living space!

Once again I was open to translate for any team member who needed me. We had our regular morning conference at the BMG district government building which I attended to interpret for Captain Dave, Mo and Bobby, one of the younger members of the new team. Other team members and village elders were also present to seriously discuss how to bring peace to this region which seemed a subject endlessly talked about with never a viable solution.

We were very patient and worked hard to get our intel information. Every day we would have private meetings with our sources and the Afghan National Security man, Colonel Nordean, the heavy guy with the leather jacket who lived by himself on the army side. He was a one man show but also had spies in the villages to report to him on Taliban plots and secrets. Nothing was easy in BMG. We did lots of walk patrols outside of the security bubble, provoking the enemy to attack and show themselves. We knew the residents were also tired of the Taliban and how they were treated by them and we also knew, by now, that support for the Taliban came from neighboring countries, especially Pakistan, and our goal was to destroy them, bring peace and then get out.

The children were always there waiting for me and I never left the fort without visiting the storeroom and filling my pockets with candy bars and ready to eat meals. In a separate pocket I carried Ilya's precious unicorn and fuzzy bear, waiting until I found the right two kids to give them to.

It was on an especially windy day in the bazaar when I turned a corner for respite from the stinging dust and saw two small children, maybe brother and sister, huddled together in a sheltered doorway. Startled they stared at me with eyes big in their too thin faces. I stopped and smiled. They looked terrified. I took out Ilya's toys and handed the Unicorn to the girl and Fuzzy Bear to the boy. "A gift to you from my son," I said. They still just stared at me then the girl child looked down at her Unicorn, held its soft white mane to her cheek and smiled. The small boy put fuzzy bear inside his jacket, against his boney ribs as though to protect it from the wind, and hugged it close. I put one instant meal next to each child saying again,"From my son Ilyas." Some day I will tell him about this I thought as I walked away.

There was not even one day that I didn't think of Rob and hope I would come across the guy that killed him so I could shoot him in the face. I was taking my friend's death very personally.

The team was putting a big mission together to catch the Taliban by surprise which was difficult as they were always on the move, knowing we were going to hunt them down. When we did corner them we always sent messages telling them to lower their weapons peacefully and nothing would happen, but some chose to fight until they died.

The team continued to train the Afghan National Army, and I reported there too.

Our tent was very close to the DUSTOFF medics so the loud noise of their Black Hawk kept me from sleeping the night before we gave the ANA soldiers their briefing. We were going to be away for two nights and everyone must be prepared for a big fight. As usual the destination was kept secret.

We spent all day getting ready for this mission, cleaning our weapons and assembling as much ammunition as we could carry. The party was set to begin at midnight. As dusk fell I saw everyone looking badass with their night vision. Everyone but me who was not given a pair of those sometimes life saving goggles. We always took two or three interpreters on these kinds of missions because we split into two or three groups. As midnight approached, the ANA soldiers looked ready but nervous, just like us interpreters. The brave men of MARSOC were alert and eager to get moving. Like always, as the pilots of two chinook helicopters turned their engines on, I prayed to myself hoping we'd all come back alive.

CHAPTER 28
ROCKETS FLY AS THE SILENT RIVER FLOWS

The amazing Chinook is a twin engine tandem rotor heavy lift helicopter with a top speed of 170 knots. Its primary roles are troop movement, artillery placement and battlefield resupply so it has a wide loading ramp at the rear of the fuselage and three external cargo hooks.

We slowly marched toward the chopper, about 30 men strong including the Afghan National Army. As usual we split into two groups, one in each Chinook, and as always two Blackhawk choppers would accompany us like bodyguards.

The wind of these choppers resembled a hurricane, and after everyone with his heavy gear was aboard, the big Chinooks slowly took off.

After fifteen minutes we landed, one chopper on the north side of a village and one on the south in case we had to make a quick exit. Meanwhile two Black Hawks circled above watching for enemy fighters waiting to ambush us. In a few minutes all four choppers disappeared into the dark night and we were alone. We rushed to climb the backside of this hill with our heavy gear. I was with Captain Dave and Joe and some other guys. Once I fell down but got up quickly and scrambled to keep up with the team. Without night vision it was hard for me to see my surroundings. I heard shots fired at us. Obviously the Taliban were already in their fighting positions but our men still had the advantage with their night goggles. As soon as we reached the top of the hill we scoped the village then started to dig trenches to hide in before daylight when the Taliban usually attacked.

Joe and I were digging one hole for ourselves while everyone else was digging to secure their own fighting positions.

Early in the morning the gun battle began and bullets sped everywhere. The Taliban always had the beginning advantage since they knew the area. After a couple of hours there was a brief cease fire while they let the women and children evacuate the villages with their donkeys loaded with whatever they owned. We watched them all crossing the river. Joe and I lay down in our trench, glad of the chance to rest. The sun was out and it was very hot; I was already sweating and I wondered how those women must feel in their voluminous Burkas.

The heavy fire fight began again and we came back with everything we had, destroying a few compounds and the cottages below us. As the Taliban retreated Captain Dave ordered that we all go down, select unoccupied compounds, take possession and set up new fighting positions and advantages. Slowly and carefully we made it down the hill.

Joe and I were clearing the first compound when the Taliban PKM machine gun shooter attacked. We dove to the ground as more than fifty bullets slammed into the wall inches away then we crawled like snails towards a doorway. All the while Joe was cussing and pissed off. Now maybe ten of us were trying to cover two compounds and getting hit by RPGs left and right.

We were situated on the bank where two rivers met and right across from us was a tree line and trail from which a group of Taliban fighters continuously fired at us.

Dave, our Captain, took out the rocket launcher he was carrying on his back and put it to good use. Now we launched rockets at their position across the river and many landed right on target. We fought all day, launching rockets back and forth.

We saw a lot of action going on across the river and in the village north of us where we also had a team fighting hard. Of course the Taliban always fought to the end, until death, and the main goal of this mission was for us to kill or capture the IED maker Mulha Muslim who we knew was here having a meeting with other Taliban commanders. We had caught them by surprise.

Darkness fell and the fighting stopped but we still stayed on guard all night, watching each side, trying to avoid an ambush. As I opened my second Rip-It in an effort to stay alert, I heard the deceptively peaceful sound of the river flowing and dogs barking in the distance. The village looked creepy and ghostly under the sliver of moon and time seemed to stand still. I shivered.

As the sun rose the enemy attacked and we hit them back harder, each time wasting more of our valuable ammunition. Dave continued to hit them with our own rocket launcher and soon I was relieved to hear our jets flying overhead. We identified one of the Taliban positions directly across the river from us and shortly our first bomb dropped on them but we were getting hit by Rocket Propelled Grenades at the same time. Our jets circled high over us as we tried to identify that Taliban's position and within minutes another bomb quieted them. In eerie silence we waited.

Recovered, the PKM shooter attacked again. Another RPG came, hitting right by our compound, shaking the ground and shattering my eardrums. Captain Dave hit his own RPGs back at them and minutes later we identified another Taliban position. BOOM! A perfect bomb drop.

It was quiet for a long time after that. I relaxed.

We started to search the village, house by house, and in one we found an old man shaking and terrified. We questioned him for a while but didn't really get anything useful so we let him be.

After this second day of none stop fighting we were almost out of ammunition and were relieved to get to the end of the village without needing any. Our ride was arriving at midnight to get us out of here and I, for one, would be happy to leave this creepy place called Panj how.

We impatiently waited for our choppers and around midnight regrouped and wearily trudged toward the open space between the hill and where the Chinook would land. Minutes later I heard the sound of two of them in the distance and when one landed a few meters from us it created a blinding dust storm through which everyone rushed to get on board. Two Blackhawks continued circling and scanning the village until we were all loaded and airborne.

Back in base it was hard to believe that everyone was alive- including myself.

I made it to my tent, took off my body armor and collapsed, feeling like a zombie after three sleepless nights.

CHAPTER 29
IS IT LUCK OR FATE THAT CLOSES OR OPENS DEATH'S GATE?

Next day we had to wait until they turned on the phone tower so we could call our sources and learn the results of our battle. In BMG the phone line only worked from eight in the morning till four pm. Taliban had made a deal with the phone company that they wouldn't blow up the tower unless it was for their own safety. So now it was past eight and the phones were working and the report came that we had killed more than a dozen Taliban, and no civilians were hurt.

The bad news was that Mullah Muslim the midget had escaped: being so small he had been hidden under the Burqa of one of the women we had watched fleeing for safety with other civilians before the battle began. So the hunt must continue for Mula Muslim the IED maker but by now we knew all the Taliban villages, what kind of weapons they had and also how many fighters. I had no doubt, even though he was always on the move, that it was just a matter of time before we found him.

I had never imagined men as tough as my MARSOC comrades were. They never complained or seemed to tire: through cold or heat, lack of food or sleep, it never slowed their eagerness to pursue and wipe out the enemy. They kept busy even between missions and now I understood why they were limited to six month stints.: the human body could only take so much without a rest before breaking down.

I continued to assist in their meetings with key village elders, Afghan government officials and ANA force commanders. I was also key in providing critical language support during foot and vehicle combat patrols so was kept extremely busy during the next few months.

Usually things went smoothly but one day our luck ran out. I was with fifteen soldiers in the big Humvee and on the outskirts of a village when we hit an IED. It blew the whole engine of our massive vehicle to hell and suddenly our peaceful morning was filled with screaming men, blood and twisted metal. Those of us unhurt tried to staunch the bleeding and do what we could for our badly injured comrades while we awaited the Dustoff Chopper which had been immediately called for.

Again I felt helpless in the face of such pain and agony and in my mind I cursed, over and over, the wretched midget who made these IEDs that the Taliban placed indiscriminately in great quantities all over the local countryside.

The emergency helicopter landed nearby and the doctors did what they could for the six wounded soldiers who were quickly loaded aboard and lifted into the sky.

Six men whose lives would never be the same.

Another vehicle came and took us back to base. Nobody spoke on the short journey but I know each of us was thinking the same thought; why was it them and not me?

CHAPTER 30
MY EYES SEE MY WORLD, RADIO TAKES ME BEYOND, TO HEAR ABOUT YOURS

The guys in team 8231 were beasts and every Friday night they held a well attended boxing match. Watching those true warriors fight each other, for me, became eagerly looked forward to entertainment.

I went on many missions with the team, and thank god no one else got killed. One time Andy, the team intel guy, and I flew to Herat Camp Stone to meet our source from BMG. We couldn't meet this informant in person in Bala Murghab because he was a trusted Taliban commander who now worked for us. If the Taliban found out they would kill him.

Mo our team chief and I worked countless hours translating between villagers and key members of the MARSOC team. On my own spare time I had many interesting conversations with the locals. One often asked question was, "Why are the Americans invading our country?"

At first it shocked me that they thought that but when I explained about 9-11 and how over 300 Americans had been killed in New York due to Ben Ladan, I realized these people had no news of the outside world. "We just want to get rid of the Taliban because they attacked us." I explained and I just hope they did understand and believe me.

Apart from the schools we organized we helped fix and paint the little mosque in the town near us. Pharmaceuticals were rare and though the Base clinic was open to all, they could only help with broken bones, bullet wounds etc. so common ailments and diseases in the village went untreated. I sent away for a case of more general medicines which I donated to the village clinic, explaining their use to the doctor, but later I learned he had immediately sold them to someone in a distant city.

But most thrilling and successful for me was when we arranged for our local village to have its first radio transmission and had transistor radios brought in which I distributed throughout the cottages. To watch the faces of young and old transform with amazement as they, for the first time, heard voices and music from the outside world was something wonderful to behold. Broad, often toothless, smiles soon took over and after that I would often hear music issuing from the bleak interiors of people's homes as I passed.

My time here with my second team was coming to an end, all these men I worked with were amazing.

I had been here for a year now and the base was looking much more friendly than when I first arrived. We had showers that we helped install, and toilets. That hated ladder we'd had to climb to go to the Army side was replaced with a gate. We all contributed as much as we could to help build the Fort up, see it grow and make people feel safe inside its walls.

CHAPTER 31
TWO WORLDS. WHICH IS REALITY?

Before my next assignment I had two weeks leave from which I heard Bobby was impatient for me to return so he could introduce me to the new team that I would work with next. It was called Fox Company and he wanted me back before they arrived. But first I was going home and this time I vowed to spend a lot of time alone with just my wife and son.

Every time I left the BMG I took all my gear just in case I didn't return. I was responsible for all that expensive equipment and sure couldn't afford to lose it.

In a few days there was a seat for me on a chopper. Bobby helped me with my load and I got to say goodbye to everyone on the Hotel Company team and wished them the best. It was like a reenactment of my last departure with the same ambivalent feelings of sadness at leaving men who had become brothers, and joy at the thought of going home.

I climbed into the Blackhawk and after a couple of hours landed at Camp Stone in Herat. Every time I came back here I looked like a cave man so I went straight to the interpreter's transit tent to shower, shave and claim my cot. Once inside I was greeted by a few fellow interpreters that I had never seen before but then a guy I hadn't noticed came up to me and said, "Hey, Is that you Ahmed?" He then said, "Dude it's Tamim. We sat next to each other through middle school."

It then struck me and I remembered him. We talked for the next few hours, even after the sun fell asleep.

The next morning I went to the Mission Essential Personnel

(MEP) office on the army side of camp to report and put my time in the field into the computer.

MEP managers were always nice to me and very helpful in Camp Stone. I booked my ticket back to the States. Normally if an interpreter is assigned to a safe place in Afghanistan he doesn't want to take time off every six months but, being in action and on continuous high alert as I was, stressed both mind and body and I badly needed the break. Just leaving BMG and reaching San Francisco took over a week due to the many stops we had to make just to get out of Afghanistan but it was worth it just to see my wife and son and know they really existed.

Besides I was fervently hoping for a new assignment in a safer location when I came back.

The whole journey seemed interminable with all the breaks between flights but finally I was going through the strict customs in San Francisco and getting on the Bay Area Transit train to Pleasant Hill. I stepped out to see my beautiful wife Rashida and my son Ilyas waiting for me.

I gave them big hugs and kisses then we walked to the car and drove to our duplex where they prepared a big meal after which other family members dropped by to greet me.

I finally had a nice bed to sleep in, in my own house but nightmares invaded my dreams keeping my eyes open, staring into the darkness. In the morning my son Ilyas was waiting to give me a big hug and I went downstairs where Rashida was cooking breakfast for us. After we finished we decided to drive around the city so I could see what had changed. Almost everything was the same as I remembered it, but all this time I could not stop thinking about Afghanistan; flashing back to memories, bad memories. Hearing the explosions, the whistle of bullets too close and screams of injured men.

That night I couldn't get any sleep thinking about the war zone.

Ilyas was still in bed next morning when Rashida and I decided to go for a walk on a neighborhood trail. It was a perfect California late summer's day and as joggers and colorfully dressed cyclists passed us, other walkers smiled and wished us a good day, birds sang and somewhere children laughed, a feeling of confusion grew in me as though I didn't know what reality was any more and at any moment might wake up in the midst of a firestorm.

We had not gone far when I got a call saying that I was due for an interview next day at a nearby army base to get my security clearance. So this would be my only free day and in spite of being invited to friends' and relatives' homes all I wanted was to sit around and be with the two people I loved most in the whole world.

The next morning my interview ended by taking up most of the day but I had been hoping to get my clearance for a long time and needed it to be deployed to a safer base. I tried not to regret each moment I was losing of my leave and when they let me go I relished every second left of that afternoon and evening. My days in California were over. I went to my parent's house to say my goodbyes and then Rashida took me out to eat with Ilyias. So short a time almost seemed like no time at all.

The next morning I got up early to get dropped off at BART. Ilyas gave me a big hug and wouldn't let go; Rashida pulled him off as he was crying. I quickly left to catch my train to the airport and as it was leaving I saw Ilyas and Rashida waving goodbye. They would never know how desperately hard it was for me to leave and return to the place of my nightmares.

My return to Dubai was just the reverse of my flight out and that night, when I stayed in the same small hotel I always stayed at, I woke up disoriented. Had I really been home with Rashida and Ilyias? Surely it was all a dream and I was now only on my way between assignments.

The next morning I took a taxi to Dubai airport where I caught a civilian plane straight to Bagram Air-field. There I checked in at the MEP office and picked up the military duffle bags I'd left there. The transit tent, when I entered, had the same shit like smell and I just claimed my cot, lay down and closed my eyes. Every fifteen minutes or so I heard the sound of F 16 jets flying over us, shaking the tent violently and I vaguely thought of the movie "Groundhog Day" and wondered if I was caught in the same kind of time warp.

I awoke to the wail of sirens and heard later that on the other side of the base they were getting attacked by rockets, which hit the kitchen and chow hall, taking the lives of several good people.

It was three next morning when movement guys with flashlights came into the tent whispering my name. They told me I had to catch a flight to Herat and helped me get my stuff together, then I walked out of the tent and drove around the base to the terminal. There I waited with a few others wondering why they always sent us so early. Hadn't I been told that the army's slogan was Hurry up and Wait?

Finally I was on the C 130 and after a short stop at Kabul we were bound for Herat where I collected my duffle bags and went straight to the Convoy truck waiting to take me to Camp Stone.

In the Special Forces area Translator Tent I was greeted by a few interpreters that I had seen before, and was introduced to some new ones. After eating and catching up on things I went to the MEP office and signed the list to go to Bala-Murghab but they told me there was only a very slight chance because they had no transportation.

I quickly sent a message to Bobby, who was waiting for me in the BMG, and he responded quickly, saying he would arrange for a MARSOC chopper to come pick me up. It was already getting dark so I spent the rest of the night talking and joking with interpreter friends.

The chopper was there waiting for me in the morning with its partner Blackhawk. There were soldiers there too, along with some civilians so I got in quickly and claimed my seat.

As we were flying I looked down on the landscape of Afghanistan, the mountain ranges, rivers and fertile valleys wondering, as always, how such a potentially rich land came to be rendered useless by the ravages of war after war.

In less than two hours we arrived in BMG, and descended slowly into the base. Once landed I saw Bobby waiting for me. We enthusiastically greeted each other then Bobby ushered me to my tent where I left my luggage and rushed to a meeting I was scheduled to catch.

It was as if I'd never left.

CHAPTER 32
FOX COMPANY

Yelling and cheers caused me to leap out of my cot. It was daylight and when I peeked outside I was surprised to see two unfamiliar Special Forces officers wrestling on the dirt, surrounded by an enthusiastic crowd. At first I thought it was a fight but soon realized it was all in sport and enjoyed watching with the rest of them. Neither man won but both walked away bloody and laughing. When I went outside I was introduced to Captain Frank, leader of the new Fox team, a tall, strong likeable guy who explained I would be working with him but until Hotel Company left I would still be translating for Dave too.

We had recently built a small building that contained twenty small cubicles so now everyone in the team got his own space. That felt really good to me and I propped a photo of Rashida and Ilyas on top of my piled up dufflebags so it seemed as if they were there welcoming me whenever I came in.

The new Captain, Frank, needed to learn what the previous team had been doing, so next day we were scheduled to gather in the small, newly built meeting room with one of the village elders who acted as a spy for us.

We got news that he was waiting outside the base on the other side so I jumped into the Humvee and drove through the Italian side to the far gate that was being guarded by ANA soldiers. There was the usual crowd of locals there waiting to be let in to see the medic and, on the ruse that my elder was there for the same reason, I picked him up and took him back to the meeting room.

It was about ten o'clock when Captain Dave finished his

questioning with me translating to show the new Captain how we did it, and I went straight to my cot but was soon awakened by someone telling me that the whole rest of the new team had finally arrived and I was needed to show them around.

I met them outside my small room where we shook hands then walked around the base while I introduced them to fellow Army members and friends. I also introduced them to the Afghan National Army guys and then to our new District Governor, explaining that we found the last one had Taliban relatives so he had been fired not too long ago. I wanted them to see how fragile the local situation was here and how they must be careful who they trusted. After that I left and someone else took over.

I continued towards the TOC (Tactical Operation Center) which was available to only MARSOC members except for me who was one of the very few translators allowed in. The room was not only used for meetings, for which there were many computers and projectors, but had one wall full of Taliban pictures and names which I tried to memorize in case I ran into them on my visits to the villages. It was like a web with everything connected by strings which we had to keep track of . I noticed one vague mention of the local drug lord.

This led to us to next day contacting Zia,, probably the richest and best dressed man in the area, and warning him to keep away from the Taliban. He agreed, promising to have nothing to do with them and I believed him, knowing he realized we could very quickly destroy his extremely profitable drug business.

That day we also planned a mission to Hell's gate where we knew the Taliban was having a meeting. As a first for the Fox team this was a tough one as no other teams or forces had ever even been close to Hell's Gate. They called it that because there were two tall mountains and between them, at the very bottom, tumbled a wild river and a small road. In my team Scott was in charge of all interpreters so he informed us that we would be leaving at midnight.

We briefed the ANA soldiers coming with us and after getting them geared up, checked their ammunition, guns and other tactical supplies. The rest of the day was spent helping them until dark and I saw all the MARSOC guys putting on their gear to look just like the

Hotel team had, disguised to once again look badass like in the movies.

CHAPTER 33
LOST IN THE DARK

Midnight and we gathered around the Humvees for our last briefing then marched towards the helicopter pad. The pilots of the Chinooks and Blackhawks turned on their engines. Everyone dragged himself and his heavy gear onboard, fighting the strong wind the Chinook whipped up, biting like a sandstorm.

The Blackhawks next to us took off first then I remember looking through the window and feeling the force and thrust of our huge Chinook as it lifted, taking us toward Hells Gate. As usual one of the other Chinooks landed on one side of the village and we on the other, I was to work with Scott and Captain Frank and as we prepared to land it was into a sad depressed looking night with neither moon nor stars to lighten the black sky.

As soon as the Chinook landed, the back opened and we swiftly exited. As always at the start of a mission my heart beat like it was trying to escape my chest. It was so dark I held onto Scott's belt. We took a right onto a small dirt road on each side of which were a few houses. Soon as the dirt road ended we were faced with a steep hill. We started climbing. The ANA soldiers were in front of us. Then Taktaktak! I recognized that hated sound of the PKM Russian machine gun as shells exploded all around us rising to a deafening crescendo. The MARSOC soldiers, carrying the heaviest gear of us all, decided to climb back down and take the longer easier trip around the hill. I, with no night goggles, lost the ANA soldiers in front of me and was suddenly alone. Blindly I struggled on; it was pitch dark… and dead quiet. Just keep going… straight up.

With no clue of where I was I tripped over a rock and fell with my heavy gear, crashing to the ground where gravity played its part and I started rolling downhill. It was the scariest experience in my whole life as dirt flew in my face and sharp stones jabbed me. Fear grew as I imagined a cliff or boulder in front of me. After a few seconds, which seemed like an hour of rolling blindly like a ball, I sensed I was back at the bottom of the hill and scrambled to my feet. After a few deep breaths I recovered enough to start jogging fast, back up the hill still not knowing where I was but urgently trying to get to my ANA soldiers. I just kept praying that I didn't get caught by the Taliban and taken prisoner. I kept jogging and jogging for my life, gasping for breath. Finally I had to drop to a walk.

I could hardly believe it when I caught up to one ANA soldier, then the rest. I talked to the ANA commander and he seemed just as confused and scared as I was. Once we got to the top of the seemingly endless hill we climbed down the other side and one ANA soldier reported seeing a MARSOC soldier in the distance: then he saw more of them. At the very bottom everyone regrouped and I know I was never more relieved.

There was a long trench between the hills that we reserved for our small group, removing our gear and lying down in it. I lay there thinking and getting more and more pissed off as to why I didn't have night vision: if I'd had those goggles everyone else had I wouldn't have gotten lost nor been as scared.

Everybody was now taking a break in the trenches and men started to collapse and come close to passing out from the bitter cold that so quickly enveloped us. My toe fully froze and I was really scared that I would lose it. Everyone was shivering so violently we decided to huddle closer to each other and try to create body heat but it didn't seem to help much so Captain Frank ordered us to get up and keep moving. We spotted a compound at the bottom off the hill just a kilometer away, so we grabbed our gear and headed straight for it.

We moved sluggishly forming one long line so as not to get lost. In just a few minutes we reached the compound, broke open the first door and started checking all the rooms for inhabitants. The place seemed deserted. Each of us found an area to rest in. I huddled in a corner trying to ignore the painful throbbing in my toe as I kept watch from a window. Suddenly the dark night started to fill with light but I didn't notice right away because of how cold I was, it was like my brain was frozen too. Something was out there showing up as a dark lump on moonlit frosty ground. I alerted the others and we decided we must have dropped an important bag on our way in. It was in our sight but everyone was scared and unwilling to go get it. Finally one of my ANA soldiers said, "I'll go." All the ANA soldiers I have trained were the most brave people I have seen.

So we watched, I know I held my breath, as he ran out the door and to the bag. He picked it up and raced back. As he entered we cheered and slammed the door behind him. There was found to be nothing valuable in the bag but it was the man's bravery we honored and would remember.

CHAPTER 34
CHICKENS FOR BREAKFAST

Once the early morning light arrived we spotted Taliban setting up fighting positions all around the compound. Soon we were being shot at from every direction and we fired back out of small holes or windows. The firefight had begun again.

We exchanged gunfire for a few hours then Captain Frank ordered us to move out and search other compounds. Some men stayed to fire back and distract the Taliban while I, with a few guys, left to go search and clear out the area as fast as we could. The only person we came across was an old man we brought back to be questioned.

Captain Frank, through me, couldn't get much out of him. When it looked like we'd got the little bit he did know we told the old guy to go get all the chickens in the village for us to buy and he willingly shuffled off into the sunshine.

Our team that was deployed on the other side had been clearing out their portion of the village and found nothing either. Not one sign of life so we decided the Taliban must have evacuated the place and gone to the mountains where they had a system of caves. All day we kept exchanging fire with the few enemy left scattered in the hills but it was just a waste of ammunition. It started to get dark and with the fear of freezing again we found a few pieces of wood and an oven like object in which the villagers cooked their food. We quickly loaded it with wood and started a fire to give us heat. It was pitch black outside and quiet. Once again temperatures dropped and we shivered. The fire only helped a little and everyone scrambled to get close to it.

The MARSOC soldiers were still on guard. That whole night was spent with everyone either on lookout or crowding around the fire. Day came slowly. Everyone was restless.

A knock sounded. Instantly every gun in the room aimed at the door. One soldier stood behind it. I held my breath. He yanked it open and there stood the old man with his chickens. We all started to laugh. When we finally collected ourselves we thanked the man, paid him and cooked his chickens for breakfast.

We and the group on the other side of the village agreed not to enter Hellsgate so Captain Frank ordered us to go search the village again for any weapons or ammunition and although we came across a few houses we'd missed previously we didn't find anything of interest.

Captain Frank was disappointed that the Taliban hadn't given us a good fight and complained about the waste of ammo. Our only find was another village elder to whom we introduced ourselves and asked some questions. He politely responded, only his shaking hands showing any emotion so, with no useful information and as he seemed harmless, we let him go and went back to Captain Frank.

We all sat wherever we could and rested. I began talking to the recently arrived ANA soldiers, most of whom I didn't know yet, and soon Captain Frank told us to gather around and have a little meeting. We tried to explain some important things like how we wanted to help the locals and get them to trust us and even if some of them are Taliban don't let them know you know, they can be useful. The very confused ANA men nodded and we decided to clean our weapons. While we were goofing around and talking, the sun slowly set and the cold crept in. We continued getting our gear together in preparation for being picked up by Chinooks later. Thank God we would soon be somewhere warm!

Midnight drew near and Captain Frank told everyone to get in line, so we all left the compound and moved slowly, checking always for IEDs, toward the open field. It was wonderful to hear that Chinook in the distance, coming closer and closer. It landed within moments and once the door was open we ran inside and relaxed to the clunk of it closing firmly behind us.

Immediately we took off with the two Blackhawks guarding us.

Once we were high enough everyone looked out the window and stared at Hells Gate which was well lit by a full moon. I was really glad not to be down there.

CHAPTER 35
A GOOD DAY

Next morning I got up early to use the limited telephone time; I had two numbers, one for Captain Frank and the other for the tall Intel guy, Nick. My sources told me that there had been no casualties on yesterday's mission because the Taliban's fighting was weak—although I personally wouldn't have agreed with that description especially at certain times when those PKMs were clattering around me!

Later that day I introduced more ANA soldiers around because new ones were always coming and old ones going. It was sometimes even difficult for me to keep track.

After that I had a big meeting at the district governor's building. General Miller and the Governor of Qalehnow were already there and during the following four hours we discussed the Afghan president's new strategy for training the Afghan Local Police. President Karzai requested that from each village ten men could volunteer for training so they could protect their own village from the Taliban. They would also get paid monthly and would receive weapons training from MARSOC. It all sounded good to me.

Right after that long meeting, Nick, the Intel guy I usually worked with, and I met with the new District Governor in private. To him we could safely talk about classified subjects as we could tell he was very anti Taliban.

After that brief meeting was over, Nick and I walked to the Bazaar where we bought a few warm blankets and talked to some shopkeepers, always alert to overhear information that might be useful.

Back on base we met with our "Taliban friend": an undercover Taliban who went by Mr. Z, and would usually come to us at night with his face covered to protect his identity. We took Mr. Z to our private room where, as usual, I gave him a hug and patted his back, secretly searching to make sure of no weapons. Nick and I talked with him, got information, then gave him some money. We had given him a secret phone so we could call him and schedule these meetings to which sometimes Mr. Z brought interesting information but usually nothing important, like today.

I really enjoyed days like this, so varied and talking to many different people while hopefully building trust and winning local strength against the enemy.

CHAPTER 36
TOP OF THE HILL OUTPOST

Next morning word went around that a kid had gotten blown up by an IED and been rushed to the army side's surgical tent. Doug, an investigator, and I walked there to question the boy as we were curious if he was working with the Taliban or just a villager. He told us that he was just a sheep herder. We talked to him for an hour but he was nearly unconscious due to pain killers so we couldn't get much out of him. They said that the IED he walked on was the small kind usually planted to damage people and not cars but this explosion took one arm and one leg. I felt terrible for the kid and left feeling very depressed.

We then had a meeting with Colonel Noreenden to exchange information, which was nothing new as we visited him almost every day. That was followed by a long meeting with the ANA commander during which we told him that we were going to take some of his men on our mission next day. I seemed to be kept busy non stop and even when I got a chance to sleep my aching back and throbbing toe kept me awake.

At eight the next morning we were ready to leave and those ANA soldiers were with us. This mission was not by Chinooks but by Humvees and M-raps, the big army trucks, and soon our little convoy left, passing the soldiers guarding the front gate of the base, past the little old bridge and then the local bazaar. We reached the famous Pathfinder hill but then took a turn heading north to the village of Ludina.

At Ludina there was a combat Outpost on the top of the hill. It was being guarded by army and ANA soldiers and as we had heard that it was being frequently attacked and a new report said another was imminent, we had come to help. A few guys, including me to interpret, got dropped off at the bottom where we put on our gear and set off to the outpost where we were due to stay for a few nights

We climbed the steep track, praying to avoid IEDs, and when we finally reached the top and saw the small building we announced ourselves and were heartily welcomed. Right away we set up our sniper rifles and binoculars to watch nearby villages.

My job was to start talking and getting to know the ANA soldiers stationed here because we didn't want one of them to open fire on us. After a while of friendly chat some ANA soldiers took me down to the little secret room underground that was kitchen for the about ten permanent ANA soldiers there. One of them prepared tea and while we drank we talked and complained about the usual things like weather and lack of free time and leave. Once I'd established this good, easy going relationship with the ANA soldiers I was satisfied that they were friendly and meant us no harm.

Night fell quickly and I rejoined my own men outside who were surveying our surroundings with night vision goggles. This time I insisted on a pair for myself too and through the night had a couple of Rip-it energy drinks to keep myself awake while scanning the area through the arrival of morning. Sun had just risen when we spotted a couple of guys running back and forth between trees in the distant village. They looked suspicious and when we saw a guy on a motorcycle driving back and forth too we decided to shoot at his tire almost two kilometers away. Our sniper made a good hit and we watched the bike slow down and the guy get on his knees with his hands up trying to figure where the shot came from. He looked like he was freaking out as we were laughing on top of the hill.

The rest of the day we spent scouting and befriending the ANA a little more. We decided to go down and talk to the people who lived in the village close to the bottom of the hill. Just a few of us went and talked to some friendly locals, trying to get information about the area. All went well until we started to walk through an alleyway and a big dog ran snarling at us and attacked one of our guys. Frank quickly pulled out his pistol and shot the animal dead. We were trying to help our soldier with a bad bite wound on his leg when a village elder ran up to the dog's body crying and shaking. We told him that we were sorry but we had no choice but to shoot him. I really did feel bad for the man; these people had so little. We gave him a bit of cash to compensate. What else could we do?

After a few more hours of walking around the village and trying to get to know the culture we started back up the hill.

After a few brutal minutes of climbing in steaming hot weather we made it back to the outpost where we grabbed water bottles and chugged them down like there was no tomorrow. It was already late in the evening so we decided to just take a break and chat. Once the sky fell asleep and temperatures dropped we went back to duty scouting the area. I grabbed a Rip-it to keep me company.

We didn't relax that whole night and all of us were ready to pass out any second from hunger, cold and lack of sleep. Thankfully dawn finally arrived, although at times I had begun to doubt it ever would. We were due to get picked up today and once the sky was fully lit we packed our gear, said our goodbyes and started heading down. With no sleep for three nights and only MREs in our bellies, plus carrying our heavy gear, we had no energy left but dragged ourselves down to the village and through the bazaar.

Minutes later Humvees came to pick us up and another mission was over.

CHAPTER 37
DONE THE BEST YOU CAN,
TAKE A MOMENT NOW TO APPRECIATE
HOW STRONG YOU ARE

It was almost dark but not quite when I got up and went to check on the rest of the men. They were all awake so we decided to go down to the Italian chow hall and grab something to eat. Within the smell zone of pasta and spaghetti we all got so excited, considering that we hadn't eaten a warm meal in days, we could hardly stop from breaking into a run. Once we got the food piled as high as our plates could hold we sat down and dug in. It took a while until we could talk between mouthfuls and, after second platefuls, to discuss the last few days.

It was almost dark and we could feel the temperature dropping as we walked back to our rooms. I thought I was free for the night when someone came with news. He told me that, at the combat outpost we set up on cemetery hill a few months back, an ANA soldier turned his weapon on an Italian soldier, taking his life before he ran away.

That news was very shocking to me, but it wasn't the first time.

As soon as the news got around next morning we all gathered outside the rooms near the Humvees to discuss the incident and learn more about what happened. They told us that the killer got away with no trace and now all the Taliban looked up to him and called him the Taliban Hero. I bit my lip to hear that.

Everyone was told to stay on high alert while they further

investigated into what exactly happened and how we could find the ANA soldier.

A team member and I immediately went to Colonel Nordeen's office, after all it was one of his ANA soldiers who had turned traitor, and we asked the Colonel if he knew anything or had any suggestions, but he came up with nothing.

After that meeting I ran into my friend David and as we walked I poured out how terrible I felt that someone I probably helped train had done this. Why hadn't I seen that he wasn't trustworthy? I had thought myself good at judging people! How had I missed this one!

David calmed me down by saying we didn't even know yet if he had been one of my trainees and, anyhow, these Taliban types were pretty clever at hiding it. "Look at the last governor, and the local police chief, no one guessed they were bad guys."

I began to feel better and we started talking about how we liked Afghanistan and basic Afghan culture. We talked about everything in general for hours, we kept talking and talking, catching up with each other, and after that he took me to his own little private trailer on the base, where I met the little puppy that he was raising; such a small cute ball of fur.

I felt much better when I went to the translator tent to let the local translator know what had happened. I briefly told him to stay aware and report if he heard or knew anything. Another day was coming to an end so a couple of friends and I got together to go grab some dinner. We walked into the Italian side of the base paying our condolences, then ended up in the chow hall.

Everybody was very sad about what happened and everyone wanted to catch that ANA soldier and choke him out.

The next morning I was informed that we had to go to the village of Joy Khoja and the objective of this mission was to clear the IEDs on that road.

Everyone gathered for a short briefing and after that got into their Humvee which was an oven due to no air conditioning in this Afghan heat. The small convoy started to move out of the base. Only a few minutes of heading to the east and we made it to the village of Joy Khoja.

Once there we stopped to clear IEDs and my friend Dave and a few others, including an ANA soldier, were sent to deactivate the mines. They came out in big suits that are used for this job and immediately detected over a dozen.

Dave took out the first while another guy took out the rest. It took a while. At the last IED Dave said, "Let me do it." So I watched as he walked over to the IED to dig it out till the wires were visible. I was back at the Humvee watching Dave the whole time but then I turned to ask someone the time, and—BOOM! The whole valley shook as I hit my head against the Humvee door.

I quickly looked and saw that the very place where my good friend Dave had been standing didn't even exist anymore. I looked up at the sky and saw Dave's remains flying everywhere.

Everyone was looking for him and running to the scene but it was sadly obvious he didn't make it. Back at the base we carried his body in bags draped with an American flag. I was shaking and scared, yet another friend was dead. It was worse that I was just talking to him last night and now back at base we were planning his funeral.

His ceremony was the next day, everyone showed up to pay respects. They brought his body in a nice casket with a US flag gently laid on top. His puppy was sent to his fiancee back in the states: Dave was due to get married on his next leave.

CHAPTER 38
OUT BEYOND IDEAS OF WRONG DOING AND RIGHT DOING THERE IS A FIELD I WILL MEET YOU THERE

I woke up weighed down by sorrow but I still had to go and give it my all for the rest of the team. We were going to the same deserted village we were in the other day and. the objective was to search the whole place because it was the source of many Taliban fights since the frightened villagers had left.

Once again we got into the Humvees and drove off, passing the bridge heading east. When we reached our destination we split into groups going cottage to cottage searching for weapons. We spent the whole day breaking down doors and clearing out the houses but all we found were bullet shells from our previous fights. There was clearly nothing here for us. We were all exhausted and the day was getting old. We decided to leave so started back to base. After a few minutes of traveling on the winding roads we took a quick stop at the District Governor's Office where I translated at a top secret meeting with the District governor, after which we also talked about what we should prepare ourselves for.

After that we got the convoy moving back to base where the gates opened for us and when the Humvees stopped and the driver said, "Get out here boys." I took my heavy gear and dragged myself to my room to clean up.

On my way to the chow hall I checked for mail but again there was nothing for me. I could have done with some to comfort me after Dave's death but of course Ilyed couldn't write yet and Rashida was probably too busy looking after him. It would have been nice to have one of my son's drawings though, and a note. I skyped home as often as I could but it was hard to connect, with time changes and Rashida's frequent trips to Germany to visit her sister and mother. Sometimes I felt she thought I was off having a good time although I expected she enjoyed the money swelling our once meager bank account.

I said, "Hi" to a few friends but feeling a bit glum immediately walked back to my room and fell dead to sleep.

The next few days all we did was visit different villages and talk to the village elders whom we chose because the oldest man usually made the decisions for the whole village. We would go in Humvees or sometimes walk, and then set up a perimeter to guard the area while we were inside. We would also try to bring ANA soldiers with us.

After days of just talking we learned a lot of information and knowledge about local happenings and, also, each village we went to was offered the chance to have us train some village members and turn them into ALP (Afghan local Police). The first village to agree to take the ALP offer was Qibchaaq and after that we had a lot of men from other villages who stepped forward. Now the next few days would be about the volunteers coming to the base and signing up.

Information was taken; like what village they came from and their names, then they would go under strict training which contained tactical and physical work.

Beyond those first three days the sign ups were open, and after they gave their information we would take them to weapons training, which I always attended to help translate.

CHAPTER 39
DOGS, TWO FRIGHTENED LADIES AND A LAMB

O ver the past few days we had also kept gathering intel on the Taliban from our spies; where they were meeting was important so Captain Frank could set up a mission to attack them gathered in one spot.

And that day had come. Everyone's weapons were once again cleaned and checked. This time we were taking ATVs on the mission with us. I stored as much ammo as I could in my pouch.

Darkness fell. Everyone headed toward the Helicopter pads where the Chinooks waited. Right before getting on board we had our last briefing and were split into two teams leaving space in the middle where the ATVs were parked and secured by ropes. I could see the Chinook pilot hitting the button then shortly after heard the roaring engine. It took a while for the propellers to fire up but in the meantime the two Black Hawks next to us rose to the skies, hovering a few hundred feet above.

Airborne we headed towards the village of Bazaar-a-Two, where the highest commanders of the Taliban, including the infamous IED maker Mullah Muslim (the midget), were reported to be meeting.

After about fifteen minutes of passing over just pure Afghan mountains we landed in a remote, lonely, quiet place. At first I didn't see the village because it was surrounded by mountains so tall it looked to be contained in a small bowl.

We landed in a distant area so the Taliban wouldn't know we were coming, but it wasn't enough, they had heard us. We all ran out in line, and the ATVs quickly backed out of the Chinook. We set up a little perimeter while it closed its back door and took off. We watched the Black Hawks and the Chinook disappear knowing we were now officially stuck here for two nights.

We regrouped and started to jog toward the compounds. All we heard was the vicious barking of dogs, and all I could smell was what comes out of those dogs. One animal tied by a chain in front of a house broke loose and charged us. Someone from the team raised his weapon and shot it just in time. It almost seemed like we were here not for the Taliban but to fight the dogs.

Frank and I started to clear out nearby compounds beginning with the house closest, knocking the door down, then clearing it room by room searching for weapons or ammunition. We then made our way to the house next to it in which we found two frightened ladies who we told to wait outside while we searched. The first door we opened it was as if our eyes saw shining gold as we looked at all the AK 47 ammo lying around. We also found a few AK 47 guns.

We came to the conclusion that the ladies' husbands were Taliban and had escaped right before we got there. We then cleared every other room but finding nothing, went outside to question the ladies.

We kept talking and talking but they just couldn't respond. I kept translating for Frank but after a few minutes it was no use. They looked too nervous to talk and they had grim scared expressions. Frank ordered them back into the house but the ladies still wouldn't go because they were terrified someone would come and rape them.

We left them alone to do whatever they wanted, but we still had to find a compound that would give us an advantage against the Taliban who we knew would be coming for us. We quickly went looking with the rest of the team and found a deserted cottage that had windows facing in every direction. We cleared the place and posted up there until the first signs of daylight, then quickly pointed guns out the windows to keep a look out. The fight was almost here. Once the sun arrived the battle would begin.

I perched up against the wall in a corner and grabbed a Rip-it from my bag. It was almost light enough to at least see where the Taliban were.

All of a sudden, as I was finishing my drink, I heard gunshots rapidly coming at us. One man on our team yelled, "Get down!" Everyone took cover and started shooting to wherever they thought the Taliban might be. I asked the guy next to me as he was shooting back, "Where are they?"

"I don't have one damn clue," he answered firing off another round.

The exchange stopped for a while, and Captain Frank ordered us to get out of there and go search for other compounds.

We all left in a rush, and went down the line from compound to compound. Parked in the middle of the street was a huge cargo truck which, when we investigated, was found to belong to the Taliban. Once we figured that out Captain Frank said, "Burn it."

We backed away from the vehicle and shot the gas tank with an RPG. The explosion was deafening and must have terrified the two women we had left in their cottage.

We now headed back toward the hillside. It was a long hike over rocky, jagged terrain and after a while we came upon this small house, all alone, sitting on the hill. We decided to go check it out but before we went Captain Frank ordered a few guys to make a perimeter and keep a look out. We went up to the rusty hinged, wooden door and knocked. We waited. The door made a weird noise and creaked open to reveal an old, short, bearded man. By this time it was freezing and almost pitch black. We asked the guy nicely if we could come in and share the fire he had going in the middle of his living room. He agreed to answer some of our questions, and let us in. We then became comfortable and sat down around the crackling blaze.

Captain Frank wanted me to translate for him so we started out with the most basic questions about the area. Then Captain Frank asked if he had seen any Taliban recently, which I translated into Farsi. The old man admitted that the Taliban had actually been in his house yesterday talking to him. We then asked if we could stay for the night, and the man agreed, going into another room to sleep and leaving us in the living room with the fire. It sputtered and sparked but soon another sound joined it. Frank and I both made guesses as to what it was but neither guessed the true source until a very young lamb appeared on the edge of the firelight and stood there blinking and bleating.

"Poor little guy must be cold," I said picking him up and snuggling him inside my heavy coat. He shivered for a while then seemed to sleep and I appreciated the warmth he spread to me because it was so cold it almost seemed as if the fire wasn't there.

Frank and I didn't sleep at all but instead talked to each other while we guarded the house.

Morning did arrive although I was beginning to doubt it ever would, We were starving and shivering when a woman came in, presumably the man's wife, who silently made us tea and then, using an oven in the corner, baked fresh bread all of which she fed to us and for which we genuinely and effusively thanked her. She never said a word, and of course we never saw her face. She took the lamb and I watched as she fed it some warmed milk from a baby's bottle.

I turned around and saw Captain Frank looking out a small window with his binoculars, searching for another village. He said he saw some suspicious compounds that he wanted to go check out so we thanked the owner of the cottage, who had finally appeared, for his hospitality and went to collect the other members of our troop.

We then formed a small group to go down to check out the new village. Once we came to our first compound we shoved open the door and barged inside clearing every room.

I walked outside into the village square and was surprised to see one man and his donkey beside a well working as though completely unaware of our presence, pulling out water to fill buckets for a line of waiting villagers. I stood, soaking in the sun's warmth as I watched, thinking to myself how blessed I was to not be isolated from the world as they were. Here, these people calmly went on with their lives while we broke down their doors and searched their homes, and days before and after us the Taliban took over and fighting raged around them. Yet these people still lined up for their water and the donkey patiently raised bucket after bucket.

By noon we understood that all the Taliban leaders we were after had long gone and I wondered which spy had informed on us- obviously someone we trusted.

Our Captain Frank was very disappointed. As the rest of the team cleared more compounds they found stashes of rifles and ammunition but the rest of our day was mainly a waste and once night arrived we regrouped back in the hills where we waited for midnight when the chinooks came to pick us up.

We tried to stay alert and it was a relief when someone called, "Get ready the birds are five minutes out!" I quickly got up from where I'd been sitting on the ground and threw my gear back on. We heard a noise in the quiet night getting louder and louder 'til it was like thunder. The Chinook quickly descended to avoid any Taliban contact and landed in its own dust storm. I looked up and saw the two Black Hawks guarding above like angels as we drove the Atvs into the copter's belly, quickly fastened them down, and took our places on either side.

The back closed and. once we got up to altitude we moved towards Fob Todd and a good night's sleep.

Ratatatat. What the…!! I bolted upright. We were being attacked! The machine guns kept firing. Men's voices. Shouts. Lights flashed across my ceiling through the space between my cubicle and the one next door. As I sat frozen, trying to gather my wits, something about all the war hubub sounded familiar. Reminding me of Ilyas. Video games. Slowly it came to me. The new bastard next door was playing a battle type video game!

I was too tired to do anything about it so pulled the covers over my head to muffle the sound and went back to sleep.

I called our sources for information on the last mission. and they informed us that our target, the IED maker, had escaped through the mountains with the others. We were pissed off that we couldn't capture him because that was the whole point of the mission: So the hunt for the IED maker still lived on.

CHAPTER 40
PRIVATE FEARS ARE OFTEN GREATEST
AS THEY MUST BE FACED ALONE

Next day Nick came up to me and said "You see that Blackhawk over there," I replied, "Yes." He then said "We are going to Badghis, to meet the governor."

I went back to my room and put on my uniform, this was the one place I could go without my gear.

Nick waited for me outside and then we both walked to the helipad. Once we got to it Nick was hesitant to get on board and I remembered hearing that on a previous mission five of his friends died in a Chinook crash- he alone survived.

I knew it took a lot of guts to board this craft but he did it and the pilot said, "Buckle up, Ladies." After a steep takeoff and hard turn heading to Badghis Nick relaxed a little but I could see his knuckles were white and his forehead beaded with sweat so I tried to divert his thoughts by speaking about who we were going to meet and what we would discuss.

A car was waiting for us when we landed and it dropped us off at the entrance to the Governor's office where we were greeted by security guards and escorted into a room where we met the governor and his assistant. We then sat down at the table and discussed many different things about all of Afghanistan. We talked about security and in some areas even rebuilding the highways, also about our future missions and plans. The meeting lasted a good two hours and I was exhausted.

A truck took us to a nearby Spanish base where we were to spend the night. Nick got the keys and when he opened the door to our room and I saw the bunk bed, I swiftly ran past him and jumped onto the lower one. Nick, grinned, then walked over with his stuff and took the upper. I knew if he wanted to he could have thrown me out with how big he was.

Once we got unpacked and settled in we decided to walk over to their Spanish chow hall where we enjoyed our warm meal while continuing our discussion about the future of Afghanistan.

Tomorrow we would take a chopper to Herat and I knew Nick was already dreading it.

Morning came soon and we were being escorted to the Helicopter landing pad where the chopper was being fueled. As we stored our bags in its little compartment I could see that Nick was still hesitant and filled with dread but he took a deep breath and followed me aboard.

Just a few seconds later we slowly lifted, bound for Herat and I gazed out the window looking down at the country where people used to be kind to one another and the only fighting was between kites, accompanied by the happy laughter of children.

In just half an hour we descended into Camp Stone. Nick then went straight to see the Colonel and I to enjoy the light hearted company of some fellow interpreters.

Later Nick and I met up and went into a private room where we had a meeting with some of the locals hoping to get them on the same page by explaining what we would be doing in the area. I translated for Nick throughout the two hour meeting but after that I was off the hook and left Nick talking to the MARSOC intel guys. I went to take a shower, because I hadn't had one in days, then went to my room, took my computer out of my bag, and skyped my wife. I told her I was fine and she told me about some trips she had taken and a bit about the new and interesting people she was meeting.

We skyped for hours until it was pitch black outside. I then said goodbye, put my laptop away and lay down on my bed to look at the only picture I had of my son. I kept it close to my heart as I gradually fell asleep.

The next morning I dragged myself out of bed. My back ached

continuously now and I knew it was from the heavy loads I carried, but what could I do? It was all part of my job. When I finally went outside I was introduced to the Captain who would be Chief of the next team after we left, then was told to get ready as Blackhawks were already waiting to take us to the BMG.

Before we reached our destination there were steep mountains that we maneuvered through so the Taliban couldn't shoot at us. It was like the Blackhawk's safe haven. Then the pilot said, "Gear up ladies, we're here." We laughed and I felt us shed altitude.

We hopped out, carrying our bags, and after I introduced Captain Frank to the future team captain I went to talk to the local employees but Doug interrupted, "Let's go see Colonel Nurdeen."

We called Nurdeen "The Afghan FBI" and I translated for a few hours, all classified information. Later in the evening as we walked back to our side of the base we ran into Saleh, one of our local spies and he told us about some Taliban who might want to defect and join our side. I would have to think of a way to enable that without getting them killed.

The next morning my alarm clock awoke me early and I grabbed a coffee and some energy bars for later. Today was a big one, it was the day we would train the Afghan Local Police.

Training these guys usually took a lot of time not only due to their lack of education but because they were just locals wanting to protect their village. Qipchaq was the only place to offer us a decent number of their men, probably because the other villages were still connected to the Taliban.

We drove to the shooting range on our four wheelers and there we showed them the parts of a gun and how to use one. After that they practiced how to load and unload and then we shot into the distant hills that had targets set up on them. They were enjoying all this so, deciding to have a little fun, we gave one soldier an RPG and told him to fire into the hillside. He planted his foot. We told him to fire, and he pulled the trigger. BOOM! The whole valley shook and the soldier that shot it, after staggering to stay upright, looked open mouthed and stunned. We all stared at the huge hole in the hill.

Then I said, "Let me try." I was curious because I had never shot such a powerful weapon before.

The guy grinned and said, "My pleasure," as he handed the RPG over to me. I grabbed it and rested the heavy gun on my shoulder, then planted my foot so I didn't fall, aimed at the same hole he'd made and pulled the trigger. The recoil had me fighting to recover my balance and when I looked up at the hill the hole was now gigantic. From that moment on I had a lot of respect for the RPG.

Training then continued, to be interrupted by news that one of my favorite generals was arriving the next day. He went by the name of General David Petraeus.

After a long day of training the novice ALP we decided to pack it up and head back to base, The new village guys got their guns and gear and started walking back, slouching from weariness, while we got the four wheelers turned on and drove them. Everyone was exhausted, and after a short briefing we dismissed the ALP guys and I walked to the chow hall where I grabbed some snacks that I ate on the way back. to my small room. All I wanted was to sleep and have tomorrow morning come quickly. I couldn't wait to meet General David Petraeus.

I took my final glance at the only picture I had of my son. Someday, when I tell him about all this, he will be very proud of his father!

CHAPTER 41
SET YOUR LIFE ON FIRE. SEEK THOSE WHO CAN FAN YOUR FLAMES

Next morning I was too excited about meeting General Petreaus to eat breakfast. I spoke to some friends who had also heard that the General was coming and when I left them I almost ran back towards my side of the base. Instead of going to my room I went to the cell phones to call our sources and we talked about setting up the village elders to come for a big meeting where there would be very high ranking people. I hung up and went to get prepared.

When the time came I started walking toward the District Governor's office. I joined up with a few team members including Captain Frank and just as we arrived I saw the official Helicopter landing on the helipad. I could hardly contain my excitement as General Petraeus came walking out with a few other Generals. His shoulders were broad and it looked like he was walking in slow motion.

Frank went up and greeted him. Then the rest of us approached and shook his hand which was strong and firm, His blue eyes were kind and his face smooth, seemingly untouched by the responsibilities of his position. We all then had our pictures taken with him. Afterwards we entered the District Governor's Office where we sat around the meeting room table with other important people and I interpreted for several hours. After that General Petraeus decided to come back to our base, so we walked with him through the little Bazaar and up the path to our gates where he was greeted by more people and shown around the fort a bit before having to leave. We accompanied him to the Helipad and said our goodbyes but before he left he took out medals from his bag, gave each of us one, including me, and individually thanked us. I was thrilled and honored.

I watched the General enter the Helicopter with his body guards, and we stayed there watching until it disappeared into the distance.

"Easy." A teammate, Doug, interrupted my thoughts. "You and a local interpreter, Sharaz, are going to the village of Qib Chaq. You'll be there for two weeks to train the ALP soldiers and do local patrols."

Doug, Sharaz, and I had a private meeting for an hour that day.

It was getting dark and I headed back to my mini room, I was a little nervous but I knew I had done this many times before so I started to pack my bags and gear. I looked over at my clock and it was already midnight, I had burned my time packing instead of resting for tomorrow. I lay down, fully dressed and ready to go.

BOOM! We were under heavy fire! We were outnumbered, The Taliban grew closer and closer. I was pinned down by the blown up Humvee as the Taliban leader came up to me. I struggled to escape. He pointed his gun at my face and I gasped for air. His finger put pressure on the trigger, he pulled it back and... I woke up gasping for air. Nick from the next room said, "You want me to tuck you in? Shut up!"

CHAPTER 42
RAISE YOUR WORDS NOT YOUR VOICE
IT IS THE RAIN THAT GROWS FLOWERS, NOT THUNDER

Early morning came quickly and now it was time to go to Qib Chaq. Outside I saw teammates getting the four wheelers, motorcycles and Humvees ready to roll. We first put all our gear into the Humvees then William and I claimed a four wheeler. William was a cool twenty two year old who loved motor cycles so I knew it was a sacrifice when he told me I could drive the vehicle—but then maybe it was too tame after what he was used to. Anyway when the green light said to go I was happy to rev up and roar through the gates.

We drove past the bridge then through the small bazaar, continuing along the dirt road toward Pathfinder hill but taking a right to Qib Chaq. After about ten minutes the village was in sight and the village elder, Rahes Abdul, was standing there at the entrance to greet us. He nodded while we passed him, which meant we were good to go.

We were allowed to choose whichever compound we wanted and would rent it for two weeks, paying the owner very well. Our choice was right on the river and once the road to it became an alley the Humvees could no longer fit so we parked them and carried our stuff the rest of the way. William and I got off our four wheeler and walked while only the motorcycles accompanied us.

Our compound was at the end of the alley and we scanned the area by sending guys to clear it, then checked the inside to make sure there were no signs of Taliban. We hired some local kids to fill sandbags which we planned to put on the roof as a little barrier to look out from.

I and a few others went to select our rooms and once we found the ones we wanted we scrambled to set our cots up and make the place livable for the next two weeks. It was now pouring rain outside and with no lights it seemed as if it was night twenty four hours. If you wanted to use the bathroom you had to share the mud with the local dogs. We ate MRE's as no one wanted to bother finding out how to cook real food. That could wait 'til tomorrow.

It grew late but no one went to sleep. Most were guarding from the rooftop and I lay on my cot looking at the clay ceiling, wondering how it held up with rain pelting on it, the weight of sandbags and men. I imagined it crashing down on me but steered my mind away to thinking deeper thoughts, so deep they soon closed my eyes.

Clink Clink Clink, I awoke to the sound of a hammer hitting what sounded to be a nail. They were still working with the sandbags on the roof and the ceiling had not yet fallen in on me although I jumped quickly out of my bed. I'd heard we rented donkeys to transport sand from the river to our compound and besides all that accumulating weight we had six army guys on the roof at all times for security. Thought of all this made the Taliban, at least at the moment, the lesser of my worries.

That day we had the village elders come to a meeting at which we discussed training their volunteers for the Afghan Local Police during the next two weeks. That settled, we then hired a man to prepare our meals. and some others to clean up the local streets and alleys.

We were building our own little base here in this village we had dealt with before and therefore trusted the most.

When not training the volunteer fighters we hired a few educated locals to open a classroom for the children and also hired women to make clothing for the villagers from material we had bought in our own local bazaar. We had contractors pave the only road and when we looked at the improvements we had made in such a short time I felt a surge of pride and happiness.

For those two weeks my team mate William and I shared our

small dark room with Sharaz the local interpreter. William became a good friend, he was young and full of dreams for his future. I enjoyed hearing about his love of motor cycles and how he was a wrestling champion back home in the States. It brought a feeling of normalcy back to my crazy world.

We would often go on patrol to other villages and talk to the people, the part of my job I enjoyed most, however we were mainly there to train the Afghan Local Police, and sometimes we would also assemble small missions to clear out IEDs or any other threats.

The most important reason we were here though, in my mind, was to let the locals know that we had only come to help. That's why everything we did was positive, from cleaning up the streets, to making the place a safe haven. We all wished we could just stay longer.

We interacted a lot with the kids. I would walk around the village in the morning and hand out all my energy bars, then shortly a whole crowd of mostly little boys, would come fighting for their fair share. We all felt great as we witnessed the village changing from a pile of shit to somewhere actually livable.

Training the ALP continued from when the sky awoke to when it slept and I spent most of my day translating. During our two weeks, we started to decorate our compound and some days went so well that at night we would pop a cold rip-it in front of the fire. Life wasn't easy but we were progressing.

Finally we made a helicopter landing zone on the open field behind the village. The two weeks came to an end and it was time to pack up and head back to base. The villagers were most heart broken, they saw us as gods. When it was time I packed up all my gear and walked towards my four wheeler. Every single team member was leaving and we gave the house we were staying in back to its owners with sizeable rent.

When our little convoy started to move, I remember the kids running after our trucks and the villagers waving goodbye. My heart was heavy as I waved back but happy too for what we had done.

At the end of the road the ALP made a check point which meant that anyone passing through that village would be searched. William was driving the four wheeler while I sat next to him behind the 50. Cal. Neither of us talked. I think he was as sad at leaving as I was. We continued on the windy dirt road until we saw the base and knew we were "home."

CHAPTER 43
WHAT YOU SEEK IS ALSO SEEKING YOU

I had no sooner taken a shower and got a meal than Tim, our team chief, came up and asked me to make some phone calls for him to assemble a mission. It was going to be another one to Hells Gate.

It was already afternoon and I was disappointed to learn that we were going to be staying there overnight so the rest of the day was spent gathering things together, and everyone cleaning their weapons and collecting ammo. We were scheduled to leave late that night and it came too quickly.

I loaded my gear into the vehicle and got into the MRAP I was assigned to. The team IED sniffing dog and his handler were sitting next to me and it looked like the K9 was more excited than we were for this mission—wagging his tail as if he couldn't wait. Moments later we rolled out of the base leaving a sandstorm behind us and as always the gatekeeper waved us goodbye.

Across the rustic old bridge, over the so called BMG river we kept following the shitty roads this area was known for. It was hard for us to be comfortable in the small interior of the big MRAP. and as my back was hurting all the time now each bump was pretty near agony. At the intersection we took a right, entered and passed through the village of Kape Baba and a short ride later entered the village, Joykar., where we parked all our trucks at the base of the hill where we knew there were too many IEDS so had no choice but to hike the rest of the way with the bomb sniffing K9.

We walked in formation, with our K9 in the lead, carefully avoiding the places where he sniffed out bombs and, under the weight of our heavy gear, the almost eight kilometers seemed never ending. Finally we reached the small village right before Hell's Gate.

We found our first compound and went ahead and cleared it. Nothing there so we decided this would be a good spot to spend the night and everyone stumbled in barely able to walk. Even though we were completely exhausted no one could get any sleep; we were all paranoid. Even the simple flutter of a bird was startling, although we knew there were always a few people on lookout watching through their night vision goggles.

Early morning had us split into two groups. We cleared out the rest of the nearby compounds and found neither weapons nor people. Both villagers and Taliban had already left the area because of the previous battles we'd had there and all the guys were upset as they were itching to pick a fight .

Disappointed we hiked back down to the humvees and climbed into our assigned trucks pissed off, it was all just a waste of time. We rolled out silently and headed back to base. The canine seemed the only one still happy.

CHAPTER 44
THE HEART MUST KEEP BREAKING
UNTIL IT OPENS

No time for breakfast because Nick the intel guy and I had a plan to go to the BMG police station and meet the new National Defense Security guy. I went outside and Nick was already waiting there on a four wheeler. "Hop on," he said and we rolled out the gates.

The BMG police station was basically a big muddy castle that had been there for centuries. The police captain was at the main door, and after introductions he took us into the room where he lived and worked. It was like any Afghan's, just a rug and some pillows to sit on. We sat down and they started to talk about a variety of different subjects with me translating as usual. The meeting was long but productive and once it was over we left and went to see the District Governor where we spent another hour.

The District Governer walked us out, said, "See ya soon," and we headed back to base.

Nick and I parted. I went to the interpreter's tent to hangout a while. A few hours passed and we were sitting in a circle laughing and drinking tea when I looked at the clock and realized I had yet one more meeting to attend. The new Afghan National Army Commander was here to replace the old one, and I was to go to interpret as they planned our next biggest mission. There were all kinds of high ranked people there and by the time it was over it was already late at night and I was worn out.

For the next couple of weeks we trained the ALP and got them prepared for the big day. The plan was to go at the Taliban with full force so we took all the ANA with us and the ALP. The ALP soldiers were on twenty motorcycles donated by the Italian army and they left first with a great revving of engines, as it would take them three hours to reach their goal, the Taliban's safe haven called Dashte Panerak. The rest of us would arrive shortly by air.

We got all our bags together and marched in line to the Chinook. The pilot opened the back door and we quickly climbed inside. The door shut behind us. I sat next to William, nervous like always, you never knew if the guy next to you or in front of you would make it. I sat there praying, praying to god to bring me back home safely, and before I knew it the Chinook had taken off.

It was the longest short flight of my life. The Chinook landed in a barren area near the location, and as we climbed out the Taliban were already shooting at us. We shot back as we ducked and ran for cover. The Blackhawk in the sky started raining bullets down on them too.

But the Chinook and Blackhawk soon left and I hopped into the safety of a ditch. We made our way to the compounds from which protection we shot back. The firefight went back and forth for the next two days in constant nonstop battle. The air was thick with gunpowder and smoke.

We killed more than a dozen Taliban, including some of their big leaders, but we also had casualties. My young friend, William, who'd sat beside me in the Chinook, took one bullet and collapsed, along with three ANA soldiers. The Taliban, realizing that we had the upper hand, eventually fled the area but I left this mission because once William and the ANA soldiers were shot the Dustoff chopper immediately came and I was told to accompany them back to base.

I found myself looking over William's body, tears pouring down my face. Tim was standing next to me and I saw his sadness too as he said, "First it was Dave and now William." My heart was a lump of lead.

Luckily this mission was able to free the BMG from the Taliban, we hoped, forever. Fox Company's time here had come to an end.

CHAPTER 45
WHAT A JOY TO TRAVEL
THE WAY OF THE HEART

I was now waiting for a Chinook to come pick me up and take me away from the BMG for good. In the last few days there had been helicopters landing and taking off members of the Fox Company one by one.

I spent time packing in my room that I was happy to say goodbye to. My turn had come. I started hugging everyone with my bag in my hand: although this place was a nightmare I was sad to say goodbye to my so called brothers and friends. I headed to the Heli pad where I climbed on board the chopper, loaded my belongings and sat down. I looked out the window as we lifted off and headed toward Herat over that vast country of mountains where I was born. Looking down I wondered if I would ever return. Even though it had been dangerous and hard I thought back on all the good memories made here. I had lost a lot of people but had also met brave men and gained strong relationships. There was a lot I would miss. The villagers who trusted me and now greeted me as a friend. The children who crowded around me saying in newly learned English, "Good morning, Mr. Interpreter." Giggling and proud. Streets, once dirty, were now clean and no longer need these locals fear the cruelty and oppression of the Taliban on their land. I just prayed the Afghan Army, now moving into the fort to take over from us, would keep them out of the area.

In an hour we made our last landing in Herat. It was always the same routine, I would check in and stay for a couple of days, running into a few friends as I waited for my flight out to Bagram. When that day came and the C130 was taxi-ing for takeoff I was so happy, saying to myself "I'm never coming back to this place." Once again I was looking out the window for takeoff; that very steep uncomfortable raddling takeoff.

On landing in Bagram an hour later my back pain was really starting to kick in. It had been pretty well continuous for some time now and when I went to the MEP office they said if I came back I could have an office job, free from carrying weight.

A couple of days later I found myself standing in the busiest airport in the world, London Heathrow, and from there, after a brutal eight-hour layover, I was called to board my flight to San Francisco.

While sitting in the economy seat for the next eleven hours, my back pain grew into agony and when the captain announced we were landing at San Francisco airport I was happier than a dog given a bone.

Once we landed I went through the customs where, even though I was in the US citizen's line, they still took my finger prints and analyzed my passport. I felt as though I had been travelling forever and ached all over. An hour later I arrived by local transit at my home station and the sight of my brother waiting was hard to believe. By now it was late, almost dark, and. we hugged and looked at each other, afraid to believe we were back together. He gave me flowers from his wife, then we got into his car and headed toward my home. All the way he asked me questions about our birth country and I talked mostly about its long, never ending war.

And there was my front door! For the first time in a long while I was really here! I almost ran up to ring the bell. Then I knocked a few times but as minutes passed and no one answered I grew nervous. I heard the lock being turned, the door opened and there stood my lovely Rashida. She fell into my arms and looking over her shoulder I saw a little head peeking from the corner. My son Ilyas dashed to me, and gave me a huge hug, tackling me to the ground. Everyone was laughing. I had missed them both so much I was too choked up to speak.

We sat down at the table where a delicious meal had been prepared and we talked about my life over there. I told them how my back was giving me a hard time but I didn't tell about the fighting, the sleepless freezing nights on patrol and seeing my friends get killed.

At this point it was almost midnight and way past my son's bed time.

"Yes, we all need sleep before a big day tomorrow."

I looked at my wife in surprise. "Big day?"

"Oh, yes, I haven't had a chance to tell you. With you home I thought it a great opportunity for my sister with her two kids, her husband and mother-in-law to come from Germany for a visit. I've booked a big SUV-you can pick up tomorrow, when you collect them from the airport."

"Tomorrow?" I was stunned.

"Yes, I've booked nice rooms, five days in Tahoe, five in Las Vegas. The rest will just be showing them the best places in San Francisco. You do want to show them a good time, don't you? They've been so good to me on my trips to Germany." She smothered me with kisses and of course all I wanted was to make her happy.

This was the first time in a while that I slept on a real mattress and when I awoke, jet lagged, my back pain was excruciating. Once I'd had breakfast and coffee with my wife and son, I decided to go to the nearby chiropractor's office.

When I told Doctor Joe Minkstein, that I had been carrying heavy gear in Afghanistan and was in great pain he nodded and, after adjusting my back, took an x-ray.

The results were not what I wanted to hear. He informed me that I have a degenerated disc in my spine due to carrying heavy loads. He told me that I must not go back to active duty and must on no account carry weights of any sort or I could become paralyzed.

I left feeling disappointed and kind of shocked. Driving home, I realized I had to face the fact that returning to an action base was not an option but I could go back for one more tour after this two weeks leave, so long as I worked in the office and not in the field. And I did really need the money to buy that house I'd promised. I had hoped there'd be more in my bank account by now.

That afternoon I drove to the airport and picked up my wife's family. She was too excited about their arrival to hear the verdict from my chiropractor and for the next two weeks I was chauffeur and host while trying to protect my back as much as possible. I also tried to avoid awareness of the painfully earned twenty thousand dollars I was spending to please my beloved wife. Hopefully I would make it up on my next, and last, tour of duty. Then I would buy us that wonderful house of my dreams

At last the in laws had flown back to Germany and I was lying home in my own bed thinking that tomorrow this bed would not be coming with me. I gazed at the ceiling and wondered what was to come next.

Beep, beep, beep, my alarm went off. My son Ilyas came running into the room and jumped on my bed. We cuddled for the next few minutes as I struggled to hide the pain caused by each jarring move as I had done the whole of these recent days.

My bag was already packed. I took a shower and threw on fresh clothes then we went downstairs where breakfast awaited me. As sad as it was I cherished our last meal together for now, but soon it was over and we got into the car and left. My son kept asking me when I was coming back and I said, soon. I stared out the window and imagined myself already living here, and that dream of the future remained my motivation, just knowing that next time I would be here for the rest of my life.

Before I knew it we pulled in front of the Transit station. We all got out and my son watched with big sad eyes as I took out my bag. It was very hard for me to leave but I kept assuring myself that time would fly. I gave my son and wife big hugs and kisses but Ilyas wouldn't let go of me until Rashida pulled him back, then I quickly make my way into the station, bought my ticket and boarded the train for San Francisco airport.

I sat next to the window and saw my wife and son still waving goodbye. The train slowly moved, then faster and faster... and they were gone. I wished I could have spent more time alone with just them.

CHAPTER 46
THE FOURTH RETURN AND HELLFIRE

During the next three days I was thirty five thousand feet in the air stuck in a metal tube. I spent one night in London and then headed on to Dubai where I spent a night like always and woke the next day to catch the only flight to Bagram Airfield. Had I really been home? It already seemed just a dream...

I encouraged myself by thinking this was my fourth and last deployment.

Two hours later we landed at the airfield where there were nothing but military planes and vehicles. Once I checked out, I grabbed my bag and walked to the MEP office to report in and tell them I that I couldn't work in the field anymore due to my x-ray report, impressing the fact that I couldn't carry heavy gear at all.

Hoping they heard me I reclaimed my duffle bags from storage and went to the interpreter's tent with its permanent disgusting smell. Someone came in while I was half asleep and informed me that I was heading back to Herat. Anger built inside me as I didn't want to go back to that nightmare, my only hope now was that I worked in the base and not out in the field.

At three next morning I was grabbing my bags and going to the terminal where I checked in, then as always was left sitting in a chair, dragging my back pain with me, as I waited for hours till the plane was ready. The rear door finally opened for us to board then we waited another hour while the luggage was slowly loaded. At last... I winced at the jerk forward as we started our taxi to the runway, then down it, faster and faster. Lift off. I was looking out the window and everything seemed to move in slow motion as we gained cruising altitude.

I was talking to the guys next to me when I recognized the mountains below which led me to believe we were close to our landing into Herat. Military pilots usually descend flying nose down and after a few more minutes there was a large thump, and I felt the tires hit the tarmac. Soon the doors opened and we got into the waiting trucks and headed towards the renowned highway one, It took us a good twenty minutes on the paved road and when the guards at the base saw us approaching they opened the gates. For me it was like déjà vu as the convoy stopped at the usual place next to the small bazaar. We got off, selected our bags, and went our separate ways to different tents. I headed straight to the MEP office so I could check in. When they told me the bad news that I was going to Bala Murgab again, my heart sank for this was what I didn't want, right in the war zone.

I hitched a ride to the Interpreter's tent where a few friends greeted me and after we talked for a little I set myself up on an empty cot and lay down to think. The same thought kept repeating, I must not carry the necessary weight for the job they want me to do. It could paralyze me for life. My eyes gradually shut and I escaped into the world of sleep.

The sound of helicopters awoke me early and I quickly got ready to go to the MARSOC compound where only members were allowed.

As I walked in the first person I met was my old team captain Andy who had also just returned, but now as a colonel. I couldn't have been happier. I had given up hope of our ever meeting again but now I had finally found him and we beamed at each other and he gave me a huge hug. I told him that I had already completed three tours of combat and now Mission Essential Personnel was trying to send me back to the war zone despite my doctor's grim prognosis.

He nodded, understanding, and with a hand on my shoulder assured me that no one would send me anywhere. "I will keep you here on base," he promised.

I got out of his office with a big smile across my face, and there I saw Patrick and Brandon, two guys I had gone on many missions with two years ago in Bala Murgab. Now Patrick told me he was training the Afghan commandos here on base and that I could work with him. I told him I would be more than happy to on the one condition that I not accompany them on missions.

The rest of that day I chilled in the MARSOC compound talking to others there, especially Safi my very good, blue eyed friend from childhood days. He was also a MARSOC interpreter but still on the other side of Afghanistan so we only ran into each other when in Herat or Bagram.

Next day I was called in for an interview with some high military officials. I told them that I couldn't go into the war zone or lift heavy gear and also made sure they understood it was my fourth tour and I would like to stay in the base. I thought the meeting went well but was confused that they didn't give me a solid answer. I wanted to be like other translators. Most who were assigned to this base only worked a few hours and then were free.

Wherever I went I ran into friends but, finally tired, I went to my cot and as always thought about my wife Rashida and son Ilyas and the beautiful home I was going to buy for them. Was it really only a few days since I was with them? It seemed like years ago.

Next morning, I got called in for another interview. This meeting was in the military compound and when I entered the main office they informed me that I had earned the highest security clearance. I was both honored and happy to get this news for it was a rare achievement and, although. I didn't mean to be cocky, I really thought I had earned it.

I went outside and joyfully told all my friends my good news. They cheered and congratulated me then, after swapping war stories for a while, I went to my tent and thought about Patrick's offer to train the Afghan commandos. Receiving my security clearance had made this one of my best days.

Finally I stretched out on my cot, thinking as usual about my little family back home, and also nervous of what would happen to me here next. I just had to wait and hope for the best.

I opened my eyes in the same spot but this time it appeared that the sun was out. I tossed around for a few minutes until the sound of yelling and running hit me. I dragged my boots on and sprinted outside to see thick clouds of smoke coming from the other side of the base. I asked someone what had happened and he shouted, "Fire! A big one!" Then I saw my friend Brandon and we both ran toward the flames. It was the ANA compound.

We ran and ran and once we turned the corner I saw one of the marine barracks was in flames. I dropped to my knees horrified. Someone held me back saying, "Its okay." But it wasn't okay! I told them that they had to go help but they said it was too late and no one could get near. I frantically asked if anyone came out alive and they said, "No."

As I was looking at the flames the medics brought out two soldiers that were half burned. I couldn't even imagine what they went through. Evidently everyone was sleeping when one of the light bulbs blew but only caused a small fire. It wasn't until the flames got to the ammunition that the whole barracks blew up.

I came to the realization that my good friend Patrick was dead and along with him, Dennis and Chris were also gone. The Colonel and I were standing there stunned, it was all so terrible! Then it hit me, how lucky I was, I was supposed to have been sleeping in there with them!

When the firetrucks arrived from Herat city there was nothing but ash. I took a good look around and saw Brandon with many others sitting on the ground crying.

The whole day was spent slowly cleaning up the aftermath. I wanted to go help but they didn't let me. I went back and sat on my cot just thinking. I sat there for hours—no food or water. The sun finally set. It was dark when I went back outside to the scene where they set up lights and still kept working. I went with a few others to pray then we sat in in the chow hall and talked in grief about what had happened. A few thought it was on purpose and a few thought it was just a faulty light.

A few days later I went to the biggest funeral in Camp Stone. As was the custom, as a sign of respect, a line was put down of the dead's boots and helmets. And I saw other names of men I knew.

The funeral lasted for several hours filled with sadness and speeches from high ranked individuals. At that point I was thinking of quitting and coming home. I was just so tired of losing friends one by one in front of me.

CHAPTER 47
REPRIEVE

Later that day the MEP manager called me into his office. He handed me a paper saying that I was to work alongside a General in the NATO headquarters in Kabul.

I was stunned! Kabul! And what an honor to work with a General! They told me to go say goodbye and pack my bags. When I got to the tent and showed other interpreters my papers they were impressed and happy, someone even finding a can of beer to toast me with.

A few days later, having said my final goodbyes, I found myself in the familiar convoy going to Herat city airport where the C130's back was open waiting for me.

Soon the plane soared high in the sky heading towards Kabul International Airport. This was the first time I was more than excited to land in a C130. As soon as the plane parked and shut down its engines I walked off into nice weather and there was a Mission Essential Personal member waiting for me in a Toyota Land cruiser.

For the first time in three decades I was happily driving through the middle of Kabul. I saw the bazaars and it brought back so many memories-and it still smelled like home cooked street food.

We entered the Green Zone, which was the area inside concrete walls protecting the embassy and home of NATO headquarters. We drove past the heavily guarded wall and past security. I remembered back when I lived here this area was known as the Beverly Hills of Kabul.

At this point we had officially entered camp Eager. The car dropped me off at the MEP office and I walked in to where the manager was waiting for me. First he congratulated me for my bravery in combat. Then he took out a photograph. It was of me in a combat zone."Why are you carrying a weapon?" he asked pointing to the rifle slung over my shoulder.

I was surprised and answered, "I don't know, maybe because I could have got ambushed or shot by a Taliban or needed to protect my teammates. Every special force interpreter carried a gun." I also told him that my team trained me and wanted me to be armed. "Without one," I told him, "It would be like a student going to school with zero supplies."

I remembered how the manager in Herat had also mentioned that I carried a weapon when I shouldn't have but I hadn't thought much of it at the time. Now I tried to transition to another subject saying how, anyway, that was in the past and, "I'm glad to be here now." He then said, "Fair enough," and again thanked me for my work.

I got back to my quarters where I settled in, excited and nervous to soon be working alongside a General.

The next morning I went to the MEP office and they directed me to where I was going to work meeting different Colonels and Generals from all branches of the government.

I had my own desk and computer and was trying to act as proper as I could while still trembling with nervousness. People came in to talk, sitting across from me at my desk, asking different questions. I told them about who I'd worked with before and my experiences. I was treated very equally there and I felt on top of the world with these guys.

For the next few days I had to take a course online for my Assurance Awareness which I completed as quickly as I could and got my certificate. Almost every morning I would walk with colonels to the Afghan Ministry of Defense where I translated as they discussed the transition of power to Afghan forces and various other issues. I would do a few hours of work every day in the office, then after that would go talk with other people in the building. I also had a group of local interpreters I was working with in their own little trailer.

One day when I was roaming around the grounds, I ran across a man, Tamim, who had been my classmate in Middle School. He was working for the British forces as top interpreter and from that day on, after my office work, we hung out together.

At the current time I was working in the General's office learning special skills and I was surprised that they let me have access so many computers and files that were classified.

One day the colonel said we needed to give a civilian a ride to the airport which was only five or six blocks away, so I then followed the colonel and passenger to the land cruiser where we got in and took off, driving out of the green zone and past the gates into Kabul itself. I was surprised that the colonel drove himself through the busy city with no problem as usually the officers preferred a driver. At the correct terminal, we stopped, and I got out to escort our passenger through security and to his gate where I left him and walked back to the Land cruiser. "Let's have a look around while we're out,' said the colonel and I was more than happy to have at last a chance to see my city.

It was like the way you see it in the movies where everything looks peaceful and beautiful with happy people on the streets. I don't know what I expected, perhaps war torn with depressed looking citizens. Back in the green zone I realized that I no longer felt back pain, probably since I wasn't carrying heavy gear but also because I was relaxed and happy, enjoying my work and the people around me.

CHAPTER 48
THE WORLDLY HOPE MEN SET THEIR HEARTS UPON TURNS TO ASHES— OR IT PROSPERS AND LIKE SNOW UPON THE DESERT'S DUSTY FACE LIGHTNG A LITTLE HOUR OR TWO IS GONE

The next day I woke up like on any other day and walked outside into pleasant sunshine. It was the time when everybody was heading to work and as I approached my office building I heard gunshots. Round after round followed. Code red sirens wailed and the base was on lock down. I ran for cover into the nearest building. I asked someone what was going on and they pointed to the yet to be finished high rise next to the base. I looked up and saw two guys on the top floor with guns shooting down at civilians.

The Kabul police arrived and tried to fight them off for a few minutes, then I heard a Black Hawk helicopter fly right over us and up to the gunmen, spraying them with the 50. Cal. That black Hawk ended the fight right there and then. In the following quiet everyone slowly emerged from the spots where they'd taken cover. I walked out and continued to my office thinking how lucky it was that the terrorists hadn't sent even one shot into the Base. Later on I heard that over a dozen civilians were killed on the streets that day.

This act of terror told me that, although I was working in a well protected Base with a general, nowhere in Afghanistan was safe, not even the capital city of Kabul. The cheerful streets I had seen yesterday had been merely a mirage with brave people refusing to acknowledge their ever present danger.

I went into the building and started to work like I always did. After a few hours on the computer I was free to go so joined some friends to play pool. I couldn't help thinking how lucky every interpreter on this base was, how easy our daily lives were but I also remembered all I had gone through to get here.

Every day I would think about the house I grew up in that lay in a street somewhere nearby. I told myself I would one day go there and see if the little bakery still made its delicious pastries. We had been such a happy family, living a comfortable life with friendly neighbors-until the Russians came. How could life fall apart so quickly? There was not one day that passed without me thinking of that house but I never went there, Perhaps I was afraid all I would find was a bombed out shell.

There were a lot of suicide bombers in Kabul, one day a man put a bomb in his turban and blew himself up, taking with him the lives of an ex war lord and some of his friends.

There was never a chance to forget we were fighting a vicious war but I was enjoying my time here and, after only seven weeks was thinking that I would sign on for another year. Then one day I was called into the MEP office. While I was walking toward the meeting I wondered what this could be about and when the manager greeted me and continued with small talk I became more and more puzzled.

Then he took a deep breath and blurted, "Look, it's not me but we terminated your contract due to you carrying a firearm in the war zone."

I was stunned. "Then why didn't you guys terminate my contract when I was working and carrying a weapon?"

He went on to say how he felt it was a wrongful termination. "But," he shrugged, "it is what it is."

I strode back to my office, pissed off and furious. I went straight to some Colonels and when I told them what had happened they were also surprised and indignant. One of them went to the MEP office and told them how this was a wrongful termination and it wasn't right to make this move. The MEP guy replied that the order came from one of the highest positions there and nothing could be done about it.

The Colonel was very disappointed and he wrote a recommendation letter for my great work there and, handing it to me, said, "Don't worry, everything happens for a reason." He told me to go back to the States and take care of my injuries and back.

Leaving my office for the last time everyone gave me a hug and said goodbye. It was like a nightmare. I couldn't believe it! I finally had a good job and just lost it to something that was not right. What they did to me was very wrong.

I went to my room, packed my belongings and took up my duffle bags. I was ready to leave this place. I remember calling my wife and son before I left. Rashida was also very angry and upset but Ilyas was too young to understand. He just squealed with joy, happy that I got terminated and his dad was coming home.

EPILOGUE

After being released from the military hospital for out-processing I flew to San Francisco and arrived full of joy to see my family. The first few days were spent doing things I loved to do with my son, from taking him to the park, playing soccer or taking him out to breakfast.

Outwardly all seemed well but something was wrong. Every day my back injuries would bother me more and more until finally I went to the hospital for another MRI. The results came in as I expected-not good. I was again warned not to lift weights and to stay away from all sports. Nothing could be done in the way of relief or repair.

During the next days my pain grew and I started to slip into depression. I had nightmares on countless nights and some days I would be just sitting there and have flashbacks, seeing my friends killed and the most horrible things repeated.

I lived life as well as I could; there were good times and bad times. I bought that beautiful dream house for my family and travelled abroad to many countries on the holidays my wife loved to take. Always I tried to hide the physical pain these journeys caused me.

A few times Rashida went alone to visit her family in Germany and the last time she never returned to Ilyas and me. Now it is just the two of us and it is officially "life after war."

Death has nothing to do with going away.
The sun sets and the moon.
Sets but they are not gone.
Which seed ever went down into the earth that did not grow back up?
Which bucket went down into the well that didn't come up full?
You've seen my descent now watch my rising!

—Rumi

ACKNOWLEDGEMENTS

I want to acknowledge Jil Plummer an author of many books, a sweet & sweet plus kind woman who is an accomplished author, a true friend. Without her incredible insight and talent this book would not have been possible.

True Friends:
George Callen, Michael Golembesky, Lyn Roberts, Charlie Burke, Rahim Aurang, Budd MacKenzie, Safi Ali, Tamim, David Barnett, Jeffrey Lazarus, Joe Minkstein, Ethan Weisinger, Andrew Benzie, Robbie Hill

And Last but not least my son Ilyas Azizi. Without him this book would not be possible and he has contributed a great amount to this book.

Made in the USA
Lexington, KY
26 October 2019